"As a longtime fan of Caryn Sullivan's newspaper columns, I was delighted to see some of her most compelling stories in *Bitter or Better*. Her personal portrayal of developing resiliency and wisdom in response to adversity is especially enlightening and insightful."

MARY TREACY O'KEEFE, author of *Meant-to-Be Moments: Discovering What We are Called to Do and Be*

"Caryn's easy-to read storytelling grabs you. *Bitter or Better* is a relatable and challenging book that ignites self-analysis as you follow along from one story to the next."

SONA MEHRING, founder and CEO, CaringBridge

"Caryn Sullivan reminds us that, whether it is a frustration in a day-to-day activity or a life-altering event, we have a choice in how we handle the situation. Are we bitter from the event, or have we made the choice to be better from the experience? As a cancer survivor, it's easy to ask, *why me?* and quickly spiral down. The real courage comes from becoming better from the experience."

AMY RONNEBERG, CFO, Be the Match

"By sharing her story, Caryn Sullivan heroically teaches us the most important lesson we need to know: Life is a choice. Every day. Caryn listens with her heart. Her book is about what really matters: caring and sharing your heart with others. There is no greater gift or message in life."

TANI AUSTIN, cofounder, Starkey Hearing Foundation

"Maybe Caryn Sullivan's choice of 'better' over 'bitter' was foreordained by her curious mind and persistent spirit. But I don't think so. I think it was a real choice—one that materialized over time and that, over and again, could have gone the other way. Her adventure is illuminating."

MIKE BURBACH, editor, St. Paul *Pioneer Press*

"Caryn Sullivan shares a very real and personal journey that will be familiar to all parents who learn to come to terms with the altered expectations of a child with a disability. I hope that parents who struggle with their child's new diagnosis of autism, or other challenge, will find her story helpful, and that they, too, will ultimately discover the beauty in their own child's different way of interpreting and navigating our world."

JONAH WEINBERG, executive director, Autism Society of Minnesota

"Caryn's candid writing helps others understand experiences many of us in the autism community share by carefully illustrating the real challenges our loved ones with autism face. Her stories of those who are triumphant in the face of challenge give hope and inspiration to many who are looking for answers."

PEG SCHNEEMAN REAGAN, parent of child with autism

"*Bitter or Better* teaches us that adversity and relentless crises can change us from a student of life to a teacher of life."

DIANE S. CROSS, president and CEO, Fraser

"You will laugh and cry with Caryn Sullivan's beautifully articulated story of tenacity, resilience, and life's often-bitter curve balls. It is easy to forget we all have feelings, failures, triumphs, and regrets. Told from many perspectives, *Bitter or Better* teaches us valuable life lessons. This is a must-read."

DANIEL SALTZMAN, MD, PHD, chief of Pediatric Surgery, University of Minnesota

"*Bitter or Better* explores the meaning of life and how the deep scarring of abundant loss can ultimately steer us toward great life discovery. The author shares tears of sadness, and remarkable reflection lending to gentle laughter. A must read!"

JANINA WRESH, Law Enforcement educator, former police officer

bitter
or
better

Grappling with Life
on the Op-Ed Page

I choose better!
Caryn Sullivan

CARYN SULLIVAN

•

Library of Congress Control Number: 2015942314

•

ISBN 978-0-9835887-6-4 (softcover)
ISBN 978-0-9835887-7-1 (ePub)
ISBN 978-0-9835887-8-8 (Kindle)

•

RockPaperStar Press
333 Washington Ave N, suite 300
Minneapolis, MN 55401
612-349-2744
www.rockpaperstar.com

To Ted, my self-proclaimed trophy husband,
who loved, encouraged, and challenged me;
gave selflessly to family, friends, colleagues, and strangers;
lit up rooms with charm and charisma;
and left a big pair of shoes for the rest of us to fill.
I was blessed to share the ups and downs of life with you.

• • •

Contents

Part Three: A Heart Too Big

Part Four: Autism—From Angst to Acceptance

Part Five: Reflections

Part Six: Call to Action

Part Seven: Moving On

Part Eight: Daring to Dream

Foreword

Caryn,

You have a wonderful writing style. Very lyrical. I've read three of your columns now and haven't hit a speed bump. Reminds me of Grisham, who is as smooth as they come. You definitely have the skills to write the book. Worst-case scenario is you don't get published, and you save thousands of dollars on therapy by putting it all down on paper.

Vince Flynn
New York Times #1 bestselling author
April 2010, St. Paul, Minnesota

Author's Note

When I was eight years old, my mother left my father for a fellow high school teacher. While Dad was at work, the lovers piled her five, and his two, children into our wood-paneled station wagon. They spun a tale for their trusting passengers, aged two to nine years old: we were going on vacation. We headed south, from Baltimore, Maryland, to Miami, Florida, and then flew to Puerto Rico. We didn't return for two years. My enduring memory of the day we left is that I didn't have a chance to say good-bye to Dad.

The abrupt splintering of my family was the first of many trials that left stretch marks on my soul; that established a precedent for making clean breaks in life without a backward glance. Any one of the crises could have crippled me. Instead, each struggle has primed me for others that followed, providing insight and resolve.

Adversity has returned frequently, seemingly lodged in a revolving door to my home.

Cancer has visited indiscriminately.

Heart disease struck ruthlessly.

Autism arrived unannounced . . . and never left.

Days before Christmas 2009, death snatched my husband, cheating us of the big moments we'd eagerly anticipated—graduations, weddings, and the birth of grandbabies. It closed the book on the second chapter couples write after offspring leave the family nest to start their own.

Revisiting the past rustles memories and pain I'd rather stay dormant. But I enjoy the intellectual challenge of figuring things out; of sorting through experiences to extract the lessons they engender. So I've heeded both the call and the pull to share lessons learned along the way.

My brother Chris and I once bemoaned the fact that children arrive without operating manuals. Cars and electronic devices have them. Why not kids—and life?

The foundation of my self-created manual for life consists of two lessons, oft repeated by my mother: Life is not fair. Don't be a victim.

The balance hails from disparate sources, ranging from loved ones who've faced adversity, to strangers who've shared their stories for my column in the St. Paul *Pioneer Press*. I've become an ardent believer that, wittingly or not, we are both students and teachers in life.

Prologue

"WHAT'S GOING ON? A nurse from the hospital just called and asked what funeral home they should send Dad's body to."

My daughter's words struck like an aftershock following an earthquake. Horrified, I asked, "What do you mean?"

My brain scrambled to discern what Julia knew, and how I should respond.

Moments earlier, I'd completed a long-distance call with an emergency room physician. He'd spoken words I'd heard many times on medical dramas.

"Your husband was brought in by ambulance . . . his heart stopped . . . we did everything we could . . . but I'm sorry to report . . . ."

I'd been trying to grasp that the physician's words were fact, not fiction. Julia's question confirmed the worst. With my own heart overflowing with shock, pain, and anger, I repeated the surreal story I'd just heard.

Her dad, my husband of twenty years, had died of a heart attack, surrounded by strangers.

"Big Ted" was fifty-four.

I was the stepmother of two young adults, and mother of an eighteen-year-old son with autism and the fifteen-year-old daughter who was alone at our Minnesota home.

And now, on December 15, 2009, I was a member of the freakin' widows club.

part
one

Broad
Shoulders

Not a "Father Knows Best" Life

DURING ONE OF MY FAMILY'S serial crises, a neighbor asked, "Did you ever think you'd need such broad shoulders?" Her question gave me pause. Periodically, since my childhood, I'd felt as if I were trapped in a fast-moving cyclone. Life swirled, then settled. I was both accustomed to and weary of the phenomenon. Yet the friend who posed the question was commenting upon what she knew of my *adult* life. She knew nothing about my formative years. Why would she? I rarely discussed them.

My siblings and I were born in Baltimore, Maryland, in the 1950s and early 1960s—the era of *Father Knows Best*. The popular television show was about an idyllic, intact family that was very different from ours.

My parents' marriage began under a heavy rain cloud. My mother, an only child, was beautiful, brilliant, and willful from a young age. When she declared she was going to marry a Catholic man, her Jewish parents were furious. So were my father's parents. Despite unusually collaborative efforts to thwart their children's wedding plans, love prevailed.

After Mom suffered several miscarriages, she and Dad adopted my brother Mike. Before the adoption was finalized, Mom became pregnant with me. So I was the firstborn, but second eldest. Traci, Chris, and Steve followed in rapid succession.

We were all redheads but Mike. He was self-conscious about

the difference from an early age. Strangers stoked the feelings when they gawked at the gaggle of little redheads and asked my brown-haired brother, "What happened to *your* red hair?"

Though we thought of him as our brother (not our *adopted* brother), I don't think Mike ever truly felt like one of us. It was one of many issues that plagued him in his lifetime.

When my mother left our father for the man who later became our stepfather, her parents reportedly went ballistic again. My grandmother developed a twitch on her face that, for the rest of her life, she blamed on my mother. Her only daughter had spirited her only grandchildren out of the country with no explanation or good-byes. I don't think Nana ever forgave her.

Nearly fifty years later, my siblings and I remain clueless about what compelled Mom to plan—and execute—the secret getaway. As parents ourselves now, we recognize certain situations warrant a mother bear protecting her cubs. Was ours protecting us (or herself) from some domestic danger? Or, was she simply putting her own needs and desires before all others?

Until I began writing about my childhood, I'd given little thought to how much work it would take to exit one life and begin another with young children: closing or depleting bank accounts; resigning employment; packing clothing, diapers, books, toys, and medications; withdrawing kids from school; obtaining and packing medical and birth records, and so much more. Mom operated differently, though. My guess is, we left the country with little more than the clothes on our backs.

My siblings and I have remarked that if our getaway happened today, our photos would be plastered on milk cartons, websites, and billboards. We wonder . . . if the paramours didn't tell their spouses or family members where they were going, where was the 1960's version of an Amber Alert? Was anyone searching for us?

The questions continue to surface, churning conflicted feelings

I already had about my mother. I want to believe Mom loved us. But . . . if she *truly* loved us, how could she rip us away from our father, away from the only lives we knew, with no warning, explanation, or chance to say farewell?

Desperate for Roots

I HAVE SCATTERED MEMORIES of our time in San Juan, Puerto Rico. We lived in a small rental home. The kids attended school while the adults taught. As a third grader, I became fluent in Spanish. After Mom established contact with her parents, I became their correspondent. I wrote letters with my new Spanish vocabulary words so Nana and Grandpop could learn the language, too.

After two years in Puerto Rico, our so-called vacation ended, just as unexpectedly as it had begun. My mother and new stepfather moved us back to Maryland, ultimately buying a home outside of Gaithersburg.

We saw Dad infrequently after we returned to Maryland. We were still young—my brother Steve hadn't even started school yet. Occasionally, we spent time in Baltimore with Dad, his parents, and his sister's family. I don't recall talking about our departure or our time in Puerto Rico. I've often wondered what it must have been like for Dad to come home to an empty house after we left. What did he do? Did he try to find us? How did he cope?

I was still in elementary school when we learned our stepfather was going to adopt us. Why? Didn't Dad want us? After the court approved the adoption, Dad disappeared. It wasn't long before we learned he'd died from cancer.

For a few years, we lived a relatively drama-free life in Montgomery County, Maryland. It was the early seventies; *Father Knows*

Best was no longer in vogue. Hippies were. Mom stopped wearing a bra. She and my stepfather occasionally smoked pot. He carried a man purse. I was a teenager. I was mortified. Why couldn't my parents be *normal*?

My siblings and I were close, always watching each other's backs. We developed our own circles of friends, sometimes overlapping, and had our first boyfriends and girlfriends. Our house was a bustle of activity, ranging from tackle football games in the yard, to parties while our parents were out of town.

When I was in high school, Mom divorced for the second time. Family and friends were stunned. Apparently, what was widely considered a "perfect marriage" was not what it seemed.

Moving . . . Again

IN 1976, single, with no child support forthcoming for her four school-aged kids, my mother accepted a job in Utah. I was months shy of graduating from high school. My siblings weren't far behind: Traci was a junior, Chris a sophomore, and Steve a seventh grader. Mike had already graduated.

Mom could no longer afford Maryland's high cost of living, she explained to her irascible teenagers. She also didn't have the friendships and ties that we kids did; she was looking forward to forging new ones elsewhere.

Though I gave it my best shot, I lost the battle to remain in Maryland for the duration of the school year. I was angry about being uprooted once again. I was distraught about leaving my friends and boyfriend, forced to adapt to a new school with students who weren't inclined to welcome a shy transfer student.

Mom argued that I viewed our life in Maryland through rose-colored glasses. I thought that was an interesting choice of words for an English teacher. Our lives had hardly been idyllic, but I was content living what I'd thought was a relatively "normal" life. She may have been miserable, but I wasn't, and neither were my siblings.

As we prepared for our move, friends probed for an explanation. Why were we moving to Utah? Were we Mormon? I didn't understand what they were asking. Though Mom had converted to Catholicism after she married my father, she abandoned her adopted faith when she abandoned him. She taught us nothing about religion. I was in the dark about the Church of Latter Day Saints—and most other religions for that matter.

We left Maryland at the end of January 1976, our belongings and family divided between a U-Haul truck, a VW bug, and a two-door Pontiac Le Mans. Tears flowed, as my sister, brothers, and I reluctantly exchanged our last hugs with the friends who had gathered to see us off.

Our journey was fraught with one frightening calamity after another. The Pontiac blew a rod in Illinois, destroying the engine. The truck broke down in Missouri. Our caravan became separated in St. Louis, somewhere around the famous arch. We had no cellphones to maintain contact. But somehow, we found each other at a police station.

Colorado greeted us with a snowstorm. My brother Steve contracted food poisoning and suffered its effects as we traversed the slippery mountain roads, knuckles gripping the steering wheels. Our cross-country odyssey would have made a good storyline for a comedy show—but nobody was laughing. In fact, my sister cried her way through Ohio.

Truly on My Own

MAKING OUR WAY to Utah was harrowing. Settling into a rental home in a new city presented a different set of challenges. None of us were prepared for what was commonly referred to as culture shock.

For the first time in our lives, we were part of a minority group. We were transplanted to a community where men (and some women) went on proselytizing missions and the disillusioned were referred to as "Jack Mormons." It was years before I stopped feeling like an outsider and came to appreciate the people, the culture, and the state's natural beauty.

My first priority after we arrived in Salt Lake City was to land a job. My goal was to save enough money to return to Maryland to attend prom, graduate with my class, and participate in the post-graduation getaway to the eastern shore. I found a part-time secretarial position with a community education program. One day a music instructor took me aside to talk about the Mormon faith. Though I was only seventeen, I recognized the irony of the conversation: as he disavowed the church's practice of proselytizing, he sang its praises and encouraged me to consider it. It was the first of many such conversations.

In May, I flew back to Maryland, where I went through the graduation traditions with my friends. Instead of returning to Utah right away, I spent a couple of aimless months living with friends, playing softball, and drinking far too much.

Eventually, Mom insisted I return to Utah, just before my team was scheduled for softball playoffs. Losing the battle of wills a second time, I angrily packed my bags and bid my friends farewell.

Back in Salt Lake City, I sought Mom's advice about what I should do about college. I had no college plans, much less the means to pay for school. My question took Mom by surprise. "You never ask for my opinion," she answered. The conversation exemplified the abyss between us—she felt I didn't reach out to her; I felt she was unavailable.

With virtually no other options, I enrolled at the University of Utah, a few miles from the home Mom had purchased. Tuition was less than $200 per quarter. I obtained grants, scholarships, and worked my way through school, earning a degree in journalism. I enrolled in a skiing class (and even earned college credit for it). I cheered on our school's winning basketball team, and hiked in southern Utah.

I met some students who'd chosen to attend the predominantly Mormon university because of its proximity to the world-renowned ski resorts. Several of the guys were from the Midwest; one was a Catholic from Minnesota, who I met in a racquetball class. We began dating. Our chance encounter would ultimately lead me to my adopted state.

In my senior year, I landed a job as the news editor at the university paper. In January of 1980, I returned briefly to the East Coast. I'd secured a coveted internship at the *ABC News* Washington bureau. I was invited to attend President Jimmy Carter's State of the Union address. It was an exciting, whirlwind month.

The University of Utah was a commuter school. Like many students, I lived at home for several years, but was anxious to have my own place. When I'd saved enough money, I rented an apartment with a classmate. Concerned about how I'd cover all my expenses, I asked Mom for help. Could she pay my utilities? She refused. Her rule was that we had to move out of the house when we turned eighteen. She'd already given me a dispensation. But she wouldn't give me money. If she couldn't help all of her kids financially, she wouldn't help any of us. Whether her answer was borne of her tough love parenting style or a desire to maintain parity among her children, it left me with a familiar feeling: I was truly on my own.

Mom's Gone

MOM CALLED PEOPLE "LOVE," in the way others use the terms "honey" or "doll." Many were drawn to her. She always set a place at the Thanksgiving table for friends who had no family in town. With five sociable kids, there was often an extra for dinner. We had two rules: if you cooked dinner, you didn't clean; and after two meals, a guest was considered family and had to help with the dishes.

Like her own mother, Mom was no domestic engineer. The house often looked as if a tsunami had swept through it. We frequently ate Hamburger Helper and Spam for dinner—with a side of canned vegetables. We snacked on Twinkies and Ho-Hos until the dentist cautioned her about the excessive sugar content in the products. We drank Kool-Aid and rarely went out to eat.

When Mom was in her mid-forties, colon cancer struck. When the news broke, I felt like a spinning top. I hadn't made it through college yet. Mom was the only parent in the picture, the glue that held our family together. I was desperately afraid of losing her.

I didn't yet have the maturity to understand (or address) the large pile of emotional baggage I'd accumulated since I was ripped from my life in Baltimore as an eight-year-old. I didn't recognize the pain that festered below the surface. That came later.

When Mom was diagnosed, we argued about how she should battle the beast. Adamant that she did not want to live her life with a colostomy bag, she refused to have her entire colon removed, opting for a less draconian surgery that removed only the cancerous portion. She coupled the surgery with doses of poison—chemo and radiation—and pushed the cancer back . . . for a bit.

Less than two years after the first diagnosis, cancer returned with a vengeance, spreading its tentacles throughout her body and into her brain. Years before holistic treatments were in vogue, I begged her to quit smoking, begin exercising, and take vitamins. I wasn't well informed, but I was desperate. Yet, she refused. She'd always lived her life her way. She would die her way, too.

Mom told us the best thing we could do for her was to go on with our lives. She wanted to die knowing we were grounded, as settled as young people could be in their late teens and early twenties with no adult to guide or support them.

She had a plan of her own. She sold the family home. She and her partner moved to an isolated marina in coastal California to live aboard their sailboat. She didn't want friends to visit her, to witness her hair falling out or her brilliant mind slipping away. Decades later, I wonder about her insistence that we move on with our lives, rather than share the waning moments of hers: was it selfish or selfless?

Powerless to change her mind, I did as she asked, though I was deeply wounded. Following my college boyfriend from Utah to Minnesota, I enrolled in law school in St. Paul and he took a job. Years before cellphones were standard tools for talking and texting, we relied on ship-to-shore communication for our final conversations with Mom. The conversations weren't always private; other boat owners had access to the same channel. It was dreadful.

In late September 1981, I made a surprise visit to California to celebrate my twenty-third birthday, and what I sensed would be her last, for they were two days apart. My gift to her was news of my engagement. Though I wanted to wait until after the first year of law school, Mom asked if we would consider a January wedding. She never said why: her waning energy and appearance spoke volumes.

On December 28, I was home alone, studying for my criminal law exam, when Traci called from California.

"Mom is gone."

Though I'd known the end was near, I was still unprepared to hear the words.

Mom wanted a memorial service, so we didn't need to plan a funeral. But my wedding was days away. Friends and family were flying into Minnesota to attend. What was I to do?

Overwhelmed with conflicting emotions and agendas, I concluded it was easier to proceed than to cancel. So on January 2, 1982, I put on the white dress and a smile and walked down the aisle— my siblings and I in a daze, a Minnesota blizzard adding to our numbness.

The following month we gathered in Salt Lake City for a memorial service. Mom had obtained her master's degree in social work at the University of Utah, so many colleagues and friends were there to celebrate the valedictorian's life.

To my surprise, the dean of the school of social work approached me with unsolicited advice. "You've been through a lot," she said, noting I had moved away from my family, started law school, lost my mother, and gotten married within six months time. When she advised me to seek counseling, I brushed her off.

"I'm fine."

I buried myself in school and work and ignored the festering problems in my marriage. I could master criminal procedure and contract law, but I wasn't prepared to deal with the conflict and challenges that are inevitable when two people start a life together. Refusing to attend counseling, I ended the marriage before I earned my law degree. After all, that was the way my family rolled.

It was years before I found my way to a therapist. When I joined a women's therapy group, I shared my childhood story without a tear, as if I were relating the day's news. The women looked at me, eyes widened, jaws suspended. It dawned on me that I'd been living my life wrapped in emotional insulation, unaware of my tendency to shut down my emotions in stressful times. The women conveyed an indubitable message. I'd gone through some intense experiences with my head at the helm but my feelings numbed. I needed to engage both.

Years later, my friend Janina asked me to proofread her master's thesis. As I read about childhood trauma and PTSD, my life began to make more sense. I realized that before I ever donned a training bra, I coped with stress and trauma by barricading myself inside a pain-resistant cocoon. I lived much of my life there in times of crisis. The rest of the time my emotions perched on a plateau, without a great deal of fluctuation.

Both joy and heartache broke me out of the cocoon. When I became a mother, I felt a connection unlike any I'd experienced with my own parents. This new bond illuminated a longstanding emotional void. Over time, my children wrapped their little fingers around my heart, producing powerful emotions that eased me toward an exit from the cocoon. When Ted died, heartbreak propelled me out of it. But I'm getting ahead of myself.

Trophy Husband

I GRADUATED from law school in the winter of 1985 and took a job at a law firm in Minneapolis. By 1989 I had fallen for Ted Sullivan, a lawyer at the firm, who brought an eight-year-old daughter, Caitie, and a four-year-old son, Dan, to our marriage early that summer. We'd never really discussed how we would balance children and our demanding law practices. But we loved kids and wanted more.

In the fall of 1990, my law school friend Liz Thompson and I had dinner with our husbands. Liz and I have often been mistaken for sisters because we look more like each other than our own sisters. But we were close friends who had exciting news to spring on our guys.

"The rabbit died," I said. "Twice!"

The guys looked at us with blank faces. What was I talking about? Liz and I were both pregnant! In June of 1991, the Thompsons had twins—John and Kristin. Eleven days later, we had a son we named John, but called Jack from his first breath. When Jake was born into the Thompson family in December 1993, and Julia into ours in February 1994, our families were complete.

Though the Thompsons lived north and we lived south of Minneapolis/St. Paul, I imagined our families would spend a lot of time together as our kids grew up. We would take vacations, have barbeques, and celebrate birthdays together. That vision wouldn't bear out quite as I hoped.

Like many blended families, our rhythm varied according to the visitation schedule. When Caitie and Dan were in grade school, they typically spent one weeknight and alternate weekends at our home, along with whatever vacation time Ted could negotiate. As they got older and increasingly mobile, they spent more time with us. I wanted Caitie and Dan to feel that *our* home was *their* home, regardless of how much time they spent there, so I decorated their bedrooms and bought them clothes to keep at our house. I also wanted Jack, Julia, Caitie, and Dan to feel like siblings—unfettered by labels—and for all of us to be a family.

I struggled to find my footing; a stepparent's role is laden with ambiguity. Finding the right balance—what events to attend, when to voice an opinion—was an ongoing challenge, and I longed for guidance. Though he dealt with conflict in his job, Ted skirted it in his personal relationships. He struggled to keep everyone happy, an impossible task with numerous personalities, emotions, and agendas in play. It was a burden that weighed on him.

At six-foot-two, with striking blue eyes, a great sense of humor, and a knack for engaging anyone in conversation, Ted made a lasting impression on most who met him. He was known for his charismatic personality, quick mind, and generous nature. Neighborhood kids would knock on our door to ask Mr. Sullivan if he could help them to set up their pup tents, or loan them his bike pump. Regardless of how tired or busy he was, he always obliged.

In the early years of our marriage, we spent a lot of time with neighbors who had also built homes in our new neighborhood. We took turns hosting murder mystery dinners and karaoke parties. Ted would walk into a room, clap his hands together, and say, "Let's get this party started!"

Inherently more reserved, I often dwelled in his shadow. In social situations, I was happy to spend the evening engaged in deep conversation with one or two people. Ted didn't get it. He worked a room masterfully and thought I should do the same. Well-read, he loved to ascend his illusory soapbox to tell stories and pontificate on politics or world affairs, with encouragement from a rapt audience. He was my self-proclaimed trophy husband as well as a devoted and indulgent father who often remarked, "In my next life, I want to come back as my kids."

I Think Jack Is Deaf

BEFORE JACK WAS BORN I accepted an offer to work in the claims legal department at what was then called St. Paul Fire and Marine Insurance Company. The job was intellectually challenging. It offered good hours, good pay, and periodic travel. I enjoyed my co-workers and liked the proximity to home.

When Jack arrived, I took a twelve-week maternity leave. Something rather unexpected occurred. My brown-eyed boy stole my heart, sparking unfamiliar emotions. As my maternity leave passed, I became conflicted and melancholy. I dreaded the day I would go back to work, leaving the little guy I adored in the care of strangers. I'd imagined myself as a lawyer and a mom. Now I felt like a mom and a lawyer. But my professional duties were beckoning, and our bank account was dwindling.

We enrolled Jack in the new daycare center at the headquarters where I worked. It seemed like a perfect setup. I could pull into the covered parking lot to drop him off and pick him up. I could visit him at lunchtime and observe him with the staff and his playmates.

The plan didn't materialize as we'd intended. Jack got sick almost immediately. Within days he developed the first of a series of ear infections. Over the months that followed, I received many calls from the childcare staff (typically at the most inopportune times) informing me that Jack was ill and needed to go home. I'd call Ted to negotiate which one of us would drop whatever we were working on to pick up our sick child.

•

"On a scale of one to ten, how crazy is your day?"

The ear infections were the first of many medical problems that plagued Jack. It became increasingly difficult for both Ted and me to maintain full-time jobs that were driven by client demands and hard deadlines.

In the spring of 1992, I was offered a part-time position at an international law firm. I accepted, knowing that part time at the law firm would really be full time (but would require fewer days at the office). We hired a nanny to care for Jack in our home. His health challenges continued.

Sometime in the early part of 1993, Jack began to change. He became increasingly hyperactive. The small vocabulary he'd acquired disappeared. During a neighborhood get-together, I expressed concern to a family practice doctor. She looked at Jack, who seemed to be in continuous motion.

"Kids work on different skills at different times," she replied. "Look at him. He's working on his gross motor skills now."

A few months later, we attended a Sullivan family reunion in Michigan shortly after Jack turned two. Ted and I left Jack with his grandparents while we ran an errand. When we returned, my mother-in-law, Marilyn, approached me with concern on her face and alarm in her voice. Although she'd stood behind Jack and called his name repeatedly, he hadn't responded. With seven children and handfuls of grandchildren, Marilyn knew what to expect from a two-year-old.

"I think Jack is deaf," she said.

As soon as we returned to Minnesota we consulted an audiologist, who assured us Jack was not deaf. She suggested we consult with a psychologist. With another baby on the way, I was anxious to discover what was going on with Jack before I had a child on each hip.

Over the months that followed, we met with three psychologists, who confirmed that Jack wasn't deaf.

He had autism.

Captain of the Ship

LIKE MOST PEOPLE IN 1993, I knew virtually nothing about autism. There were no cover spreads in magazines offering personal stories or updates on genetics research. I'd seen *Rain Man*, the 1988 film in which Dustin Hoffman portrayed a man with autism, but that was the extent of my awareness of a condition that affected one in ten thousand at the time. Yet, I knew we were dealing with a far more serious concern than Jack's chronic ear infections.

Ted was more informed. As a college student, he'd worked with individuals with autism who were extremely challenged. Given his experience, he worried we might have to put Jack into an institution. Horrified, I told him to never mention that prospect again. He didn't.

As the gravity of the diagnosis took hold, my brain seemed to barricade itself from the word to insulate me from the devastating news. I couldn't utter the word "autism" for months.

We enlisted the expertise of a team of psychologists, speech therapists, and teachers to educate us and to formulate a plan of action. The process was overwhelming—and bruising—as professionals offered their interpretations of Jack's failure to make eye contact, to sustain his attention, to speak, or to engage in age-appropriate play.

The first psychologist, a family therapist, attributed Jack's condition to "a history of emotional neglect" because Ted and I worked at demanding jobs, and I took business calls on weekdays when I was at home. During our visits, she observed our two-year-old's impulsive behavior and imputed my parenting: Jack reached for the telephone on her desk because he had been wondering where I was during the work day; he tossed a baby bottle in the wastebasket because he had difficulty breast feeding; and he crawled under the office rug because he was searching for me.

I was increasingly troubled by our encounters with this "expert." When she asked me to schedule an appointment with her to discuss my relationship with my mother, I was aghast. Admittedly, I had unresolved issues with my deceased mother. But how would a therapy session about *her* help my son regain his speech?

Ted and I had fierce arguments about the therapist's request. He wanted me to comply. I countered that it was easy for him to take that position; after all, she hadn't asked to discuss *his* relationship with *his* mother!

I was a new parent with tender emotions, but good instincts. Believing our encounters with the family therapist were more harmful than helpful, I decided to pull the plug.

The therapist I'd come to loathe made another shocking statement. If we took a break from her therapy sessions, she warned, we wouldn't be welcome to return. Though she was a psychologist, she didn't understand a fundamental rule of human nature: don't piss off a redhead.

We left and never returned.

The second psychologist was renowned for her expertise with developmental disorders and autism, even before the condition burgeoned. She made time in her busy schedule to evaluate Jack shortly before Julia was born. She quickly debunked the "refrigerator mother theory" to which the family therapist ascribed. Jack's autism was *not* due to emotional neglect or a failure to bond.

More comfortable with her, I pressed for a prognosis. How long would Jack's autism last? What would his life look like? She wouldn't wager an opinion.

We got along well until she described Jack as being *disabled*.

Distraught, I pushed back. It was one thing to describe my son as having developmental delays; it was quite another to refer to him as being disabled. Having grown up before people with disabilities were mainstreamed, I had little understanding about their lives or their challenges. But there was something about the word that sounded and felt so . . . hopeless.

With the diagnosis still fresh, I became an advocate for my son. Years before I heard others use the words, I insisted Jack was not *disabled*; he was just *differently abled*.

We met with a third psychologist to learn about a therapy called applied behavioral analysis (ABA). The specialist told us if Jack, nearly three, progressed on his current trajectory, he would be "normal" by high school. I finally had a prognosis! And a goal. I would eliminate the unwelcome condition that had stolen my child, as well as dreams of the "normal" family I yearned for.

We tried ABA, with no success. One day Jack was wandering around our backyard with the woman we'd hired to work with him on the behavioral program. He wasn't cooperating with her requests, and she was frustrated. When I asked her why she was having such difficulty engaging him, she shocked me with her response.

"People with autism are just lazy."

What?

I was taking the first steps on my journey of discovery about autism. But I knew that Jack wasn't lazy. Something was off; but that explanation was shocking and offensive.

We moved on—again.

I realized I was the captain of the ship, and I had a lot to learn. I put on my captain's cap and embarked on an exhaustive, and exhausting, journey to right the ship.

From Business Suits to Sweat Suits

I HAD NO PLAN, only a burning call to action, when, in October 1993, I tearfully told my colleagues I needed to step away from the firm to address my son's needs. It was a tough decision. I've never regretted it.

Ted was not pleased. He was proud to have a professional spouse and relied upon two incomes to pay for our five-bedroom home. But I was unwavering.

Though I was resolved about my mission, I was completely unprepared to swap my business suit for sweatpants. Being a suburban stay-at-home mom was the antithesis of how I was raised by my liberal mother. I hadn't anticipated I would experience an identity crisis.

After years of easily answering questions about what I did for a living, I struggled to describe my new role. Housewife? Stay-at-home mom? I labored to say the words I'd never imagined would cross my lips.

Eventually I found a new identity when I joined the growing ranks of autism moms also committed to unraveling the autism mystery and vanquishing it from our lives. My world contracted as Jack's needs grew. My professional relationships evaporated. I didn't hear from my former colleagues. I'd left the fraternity; I felt forgotten. It smarted.

My social network became a close circle of women who lived nearby. Notions of spending time with the Thompson family didn't materialize as I'd imagined; our kids' lives took dramatically different directions. Instead of sharing experiences, I shared my woes with Liz over the telephone. She was a patient and faithful confidant.

Professionals stressed the importance of early intervention strategies to help Jack regain the speech he'd lost before his second birthday, develop the fine motor skills that eluded him, learn social cues, and establish eye contact. I took him to therapists and medical practitioners to address a growing constellation of needs.

I joined online groups, attended conferences, and devoured books. The school district assigned an amazing teacher who came to our home a few hours per week. Susan was a bright light during a frightening and confusing time. She worked with Jack in our home and often took him to her own house so he could interact with her children while we took a break from the busy boy we called Jumping Jack Flash.

The more I learned about autism, the more I worried about how I could meet everyone's needs. There was so much to be done to help Jack. How would I be able to care for our newborn, not to mention the rest of the family? My friend Jacque assured me that everyone would get what they needed. I wasn't so sure.

Jack had lost his language, but he was also very delayed in developing skills most people take for granted—eating, sleeping, using the toilet, and making friends. His needs were overwhelming, my desire to fix them intense. If there was a rationale for trying a therapy, mainstream medical or homeopathic treatment, I went all in, sometimes to Ted's dismay. His critical mind could be more objective than my desperate heart. Time and money became irrelevant. Getting our boy back was my single most important objective.

Ted was often frustrated by my immersion in my goal. I was irritated that he ignored the pile of reading materials I set on his nightstand. He preferred to read the *Wall Street Journal,* or the sports section of the newspaper. We were forging our own paths, and we weren't always particularly happy with each other about it.

Ted spent a lot of time with Jack when he was home. He accompanied us to medical appointments when Jack went under anesthesia to have his teeth cleaned or his ear tubes inserted, and attended endless conferences with the teams that developed over the years. One day Ted explained why he wouldn't read the articles about autism. As soon as he had learned of Jack's diagnosis, he told me, he realized he would be working the rest of his life to support him. He was as informed as he needed to be. The research and advocacy was my bailiwick. That conversation helped to clear the angst that had begun to wedge its way between us.

In time, Ted's unhappiness about my decision to retire gave way. He recognized it would have been impossible for us to balance two demanding careers and an equally demanding home life. He began to refer to me with pride as the CEO of Sullivan, Inc. I managed the home, while he immersed himself at work to pay the bills, and to save for an indeterminate future with the boy we cherished, though he drove us to distraction.

Looking back, I wonder how much my determination to fix Jack was driven by an unconscious need to disprove the psychologist who had accused me of emotional neglect. I desperately wanted to realize the behaviorist's inference that Jack might be "normal" by high school; to shield him from wearing the term "disabled" like a cloak, and to reclaim the life I'd imagined he (we) would lead.

Life has always been an adventure with the guy who pulled the fire alarm in first grade because it said, "pull down." He's a concrete thinker who speaks his mind. In a world where many make self-serving statements or confabulate, my son speaks the truth. He has bettered my life in ways I could never have imagined. No person, experience, or interaction in my life has had as enduring and profound an impact as our Jumping Jack Flash.

It's Not Heartburn

PRESIDENT BILL CLINTON'S PROBLEMS with women had not only captured media attention, they had made their way into the court system. In October 1998, the Eight Circuit Court of Appeals convened in St. Paul to consider Paula Jones' sexual harassment case. My husband, a self-proclaimed "recovering Democrat," decided to attend.

Ted inhaled a hot dog for lunch as he raced from his Minneapolis law office to the St. Paul courthouse. Though he later joked it was the oral argument that made him ill, he felt enough discomfort in his chest to leave the courthouse and drive to a nearby emergency room. Routine tests provided no answers. The doctor diagnosed heartburn and sent him home.

The next day Ted decided to go for a run after work. He went to his favorite spot along the Mississippi River in St. Paul, ran a few miles, came home, and stretched out on the bed. The "heartburn" he'd experienced the previous day was back. Over the course of the evening, Ted's symptoms progressed. I called Dr. Jim Thompson, go-to guy for after-hours medical advice. Reluctant to return to the emergency room, Ted decided to wait and check in with Jim periodically. As our pillar of strength lay on the bed in pain, my own heart began to beat faster. Not one to become hysterical, I watched with increasing concern as his chest felt tighter and breathing became more labored.

We decided to wait for Dan to return from a basketball game so Jack and Julia wouldn't be alone. Then we'd go to the ER. As the

10:00 p.m. news broadcasts ramped up, our anxiety followed suit. We should have called an ambulance and arranged for a neighbor to stay with Jack and Julia. But paramedics and ambulances are for dire situations, and Ted ran marathons . . . and he was healthy . . . and his symptoms weren't *that* serious—or so we believed. The minute Dan pulled into the driveway, I hustled Ted into my vehicle and headed straight to the hospital he had visited a day earlier.

In the wee hours of the morning, an enzyme test confirmed Ted had suffered a heart attack. We were in shock. He was forty-three. He had no family history of heart disease and had quit smoking years earlier. Absent an alternative explanation, we blamed stress. After all, he left home each morning for a pressure-filled job driven by clients' needs and court deadlines. He returned at night to an exhausted wife who often hadn't started dinner and couldn't wait to pass off the kids.

With Ted lying in the cardiac intensive care unit, I overheard a doctor speaking to the patient in the next room. From what I could discern, the man was an overweight, beer-drinking laborer in his thirties. If he didn't change his lifestyle, the doctor stressed, he might not survive another heart attack. Though my husband hadn't gotten the same lecture, I was scared to death.

Ted spent a few days recuperating before he stepped back into work as if he'd suffered from just another sinus infection. When a heart gives out, it's natural to be fearful and depressed. I was. Though he was reticent, Ted was, too.

Hope that the heart attack was an anomaly was short lived. In the years that followed, Ted's law practice took him around the country and the world. His heart took him back to the cardiology unit. He never abandoned his trademark humor as he acquired one, two, three, four, five, six, seven stents. He became a familiar patient, often using a favorite line on unsuspecting anesthesiologists and cardiologists: "Hey, doc, are you going to give me the penile implant while I'm under?"

I'm Not Going to Die From This

TED WASN'T THE ONLY MAN in my life to deal with health challenges at an early age. I was thirteen when I learned my father had died of cancer at age forty-three. We never really knew why. We'd spent limited time with him after we returned to Maryland from Puerto Rico. Had he already known he was sick then? If so, he didn't let on, because his death came as a complete shock to us.

News of his death sparked a debate about whether we would attend the funeral. Logistics were problematic. Dad's mother would never forgive Mom for spiriting us out of the country with no warning. She was adamant that her former daughter-in-law not attend the funeral. The adults being incapable of putting aside their differences, Dad was buried in a Baltimore cemetery without us in attendance. With no opportunity to grieve, we moved on, as we always did, with little contact with Dad's family thereafter.

Given my parents' medical histories, I began getting colonoscopies at thirty-five. I was diligent about getting annual physicals. I wanted to take my own health concerns off the list of what could go wrong.

In 2003, Caitie and Dan were finishing college and high school, respectively. Jack was in middle school and Julia in elementary school. As an owner of the law firm, Ted was focused on generating and retaining clients, supervising associate attorneys, dealing with business issues, and managing a demanding caseload. I continued to be the family CEO.

Sometime that winter, I told my brother Steve that I felt something festering inside me and feared I was getting sick. In early April 2003, I felt a sharp pain in my breast as I was walking toward the stairs. When I touched the source of the pain, I felt something hard, about the size of a pea. What the hell? I'd had a clear mammogram a few months earlier.

When I told Ted, his response was "I don't care what you have planned tomorrow, you are going to the doctor." But it was unnecessary. Something was amiss. I cope and I survive, but I need facts. Off to the doctor I went.

I met with my internist, who also felt the lump. After another clear mammogram she ordered an ultrasound, which was a bit more revealing. When the radiologist offered to schedule a biopsy for me early the following week, my stomach did a cartwheel. I pressed his assistant.

"Is he just a really nice guy, or did he not like what he saw?"

With her eyes averted, she hesitated before she replied, "A little of both."

I left the clinic in a daze, convinced I had cancer. But breast cancer? Where did that come from?

Ted was a wreck while we awaited the biopsy results. When we didn't hear from my internist, he called her at home. She confirmed I had Stage I breast cancer. I was surprisingly calm, but steadfast. "I'm not going to die from this." I was forty-four. I'd spent too many years without parents; I wasn't going to let my children suffer the same fate. I went into familiar territory, gathering information so I could formulate a plan of action . . . all without letting emotions get a foot in the door.

I was referred to the Piper Cancer Institute in Minneapolis. The radiologist was exceedingly thorough. She ran scans of both breasts and armpits, then scheduled an MRI that revealed five lumps—none of which had been detected by the mammogram, and only one that appeared in the first ultrasound. My surgeon reviewed my risks and options and referred me to the other members of my treatment team. Facts in hand, it was time to evaluate options and make plans.

After my diagnosis, Caitie gave me a book titled *Angels and Bolters*. The author, Dr. Karen Ritchie, describes four types of "creatures" that patients encounter as they undergo their cancer experience.

Preachers, the psychiatrist explains, are the people who eagerly impart advice and information. They promote resources they are convinced will work—but only if the patient uses them properly.

The clueless are the folks who make inane comments often founded on their own fears. They are concerned for their own welfare—and the patient's—in that order. They need the world to make sense, so they suggest the patient caused her own cancer, or that it's not that big a deal to lose your hair.

The bolters are the people who disappear. They can't cope with sadness or mortality.

Angels are the folks who intuitively know what to do and say. They walk your dog, or drop by with coffee just to listen and keep you company.

Fellow travelers are the folks who share your journey. They may be on the journey out of desire or necessity (spouses, for example). They may or may not know how to be supportive, but they do try.

I read *Angels and Bolters* when I was undergoing my treatment. Years later I revisited it and concluded that the premise applies to more than cancer patients. I've experienced angels and bolters during every one of my crises.

Chemo and Mortar Boards

NEARLY EVERYONE I KNEW had a friend, sister, or neighbor who had dealt with breast cancer, with mixed results. I inhaled news of positive outcomes. I wondered why anyone would tell me about anything else. Apparently, they were the "clueless" folks Dr. Ritchie described.

I conferred with fellow travelers about whether to undergo a single or double mastectomy, ultimately opting for the latter. I couldn't imagine having my body so dramatically altered, but it was inevitable.

A double mastectomy would assuage concerns of a cancer recurrence. It meant I'd never again have my breasts smushed into a cold piece of medical equipment by a stranger. It ensured that, years hence, I wouldn't look in the mirror and see one perky and one droopy breast. Although it was a difficult decision to make at the time, it's one I've never regretted.

As people flocked to my side, Ted and my kids received considerably less attention. One day, a fellow traveler called with an offer. When she was diagnosed with cancer, Wendy explained, few people asked how her husband Tim was faring. Wendy was calling on Tim's behalf to say he'd be happy to talk with Ted if he was so inclined.

Kids have their own way of dealing with illness and death, but in the midst of our own crises we can overlook their needs. My kids didn't display outward signs of fear or concern, though they likely harbored them. Julia later reported she wasn't worried because I wasn't worried, but she was a little freaked out after my surgery.

Over the course of the month that separated my diagnosis and my surgery, I discussed options and made plans. I taxed my problem-solving mind and ignored my feelings.

On May 1, 2003, cancer was no longer a problem to be solved, but an experience to be endured. I was heading to the hospital so strangers could cut off the most personal parts of my body and replace them with man-made proxies.

As I was packing my overnight bag, fear lost patience. With Ted holding me up, I sobbed away a month's worth of fear, anger, and despair. When I checked into the hospital an hour later, I was cried out, but determined.

Two weeks after my surgery, I accompanied Ted to Lawrence, Kansas. I had a pale complexion; drains hung from the sides of the reconstructed breasts beneath my blouse. Life was marching on; I wasn't going to miss Caitie's college graduation. Nor would I miss Dan's graduation from St. Thomas Academy soon after.

With the graduations behind us, I began the next phase of my treatment in June. My Stage I diagnosis allowed me to choose between two chemo cocktails. One would cause my hair to fall out; the other would not. I opted for the drugs that would attack cancer cells but leave my hair intact. There wasn't much difference in the outcome, and the chemo was basically preventative.

My kids seemed to have taken the news of my cancer well. I didn't want to upset them by losing my hair, or so I said. I knew vanity drove my decision. It was hard enough to lose my breasts. I didn't want to lose my hair, too.

Friends and neighbors rallied and brought meals. I spent hours in the oncology clinic wondering how I ended up among older, sicker patients with no hair on their heads. I felt sorry for them. It didn't occur to me they might look at the much younger woman with an IV protruding from her arm with similar sentiments.

The day after my forty-fifth birthday, I had my final chemo treatment. I prayed I'd never see an IV again. But it was not to be. Though I'd feared my siblings or I would get sick, I never imagined that our perpetually healthy ten-year-old would develop a rare and deadly disease and undergo chemo before she hit puberty.

part
two

*Life
in Limbo*

Horses and Zebras

TEN MONTHS after I completed my chemotherapy, Julia began a slow decline from an Energizer bunny to a zombie in pajamas. As I recouped my strength, she lost hers. Like Caitie and Dan, she had been a healthy child. Yet after she returned from summer camp in 2004, she began to complain of headaches and fatigue. We were in and out of the pediatrician's office as Dr. Jim ruled out culprits like Lyme's disease and said she was likely suffering from a virus.

By late fall, Julia's headaches were excruciating. We were scheduled for a Disney World getaway with Ted's mother and his sister Therese's family in early December. Concerned about whether Julia could handle the trip, I took her to see a neurologist in St. Paul, who examined her, then declared, "This child is very sick. She needs to be admitted to the hospital immediately."

While Ted and Jack went on the Disney adventure, Julia and I went to St. Paul Children's Hospital. Separated by more than a thousand miles, we all had drama-filled weekends.

The excitement began in Orlando almost immediately. As Ted was checking into the hotel, Jack disappeared. This wasn't the first time he'd wandered off. He was prone to disappearing when something caught his attention: at the Spy Museum in Washington, DC, or the Renaissance Festival near our home.

Though it was his first trip to Disney World, our thirteen-year-old had an internal GPS that led him straight to the video games. A frantic search ended when his Uncle Ron located him in the arcade—the logical place to search for him. Like many on the autism spectrum, Jack had certain fixations; video games was one of them. Follow the fixation, find the runaway.

The drama continued the following day when Grandma Marilyn fainted in the Florida heat. Jack added levity to an unnerving moment when he instructed the first responders, "Take my grandma to the Mickey Mouse infirmary and get her the best medical care Disney World has to offer."

Meanwhile in St. Paul, the physicians gathered around Julia. Our pediatrician, an infectious disease specialist, a hematology/oncology doctor, and the neurologist conferred, ran more tests, and ultimately discharged Julia with no diagnosis, but with a follow-up appointment at the hematology/oncology clinic.

Like the sharp pain that led to my cancer diagnosis, Julia's headaches led her to the neurologist, who played a crucial role in moving us toward a diagnosis.

I have enormous respect for medical professionals. But not all of them have the same skill or bedside manner. The neurologist was arrogant and dogmatic, frequently reminding me that she was the doctor, and I was the mother. Her style of doctoring had been common when I was a child. But times had changed. I am an independent-thinking consumer of medical services. If a physician or medical facility is not a good fit, I have no qualms about moving on.

When the neurologist threw down a gauntlet—if I didn't follow her instructions, she would not treat Julia any longer—I realized she didn't understand about redheads and temperament . . . .

We moved on.

Once Julia was a patient in the hematology/oncology clinic, the conversations varied from frustrating to terrifying. One doctor said Julia didn't look *that sick*. Then he ran more tests and began to prepare us for diagnoses that never panned out. Julia continued to attend school and play hockey, though her headaches worsened, her golden complexion paled, and her trim physique began to slump.

·

As the year drew to a close, we were referred to Dr. Susan Sencer to discuss a nutritional concern. She was part of the hematology/oncology group, but knew more about nutrition than her colleagues. After taking a history and conducting an exam, Dr. Sencer left the examining room. Periodically, she returned with new questions.

I've since learned that, in their training, doctors are taught to look for horses, not zebras. In the course of our lengthy visit with Dr. Sencer, it became clear the search for horses had ended.

In January 2005, we learned Julia had a zebra. Her zebra was a disease I could barely pronounce: paroxysmal nocturnal hemoglobinuaria (PNH). PNH is a rare, genetically acquired disease involving the breakdown of red blood cells. Though it afflicts more adults than children, it had put our fifth-grader's life in peril.

Jackpot

WITH BAD LUCK breathing down our necks, I learned to appreciate anything that worked in Julia's favor. We were fortunate that another hematology/oncology doctor at Children's had worked at Duke University, one of the medical centers with experience with PNH at that time.

Sporting his trademark bow tie, Dr. Steve Nelson counseled us on Julia's treatment options, grim and risky. They could treat the PNH with medications and blood transfusions. She would be susceptible to potentially fatal blood clots. She would not be able to play her favorite sports—hockey and soccer—because they involved too much contact. Her life expectancy would be unspeakably short. Nothing about that option was appealing, especially not to Julia who loved to play hockey.

The other alternative was a bone marrow transplant. *A what?* A BMT, we learned, required a donor, preferably one who was perfectly matched. A blood test can determine whether two people share sufficient levels of HLA (human leukocyte antigen) for one to donate bone marrow to the other.

Since a sibling was our best shot, I took both Jack and Julia to the hospital for testing. Despite his fear of needles, Jack, thirteen, submitted to the procedure, squeezing my hand until it went numb. We didn't get into specifics about what he was being tested for. In his typical fashion, Jack gleaned enough information from the conversations to put it into context for himself.

On our way home from the hospital, Jack looked up from his handheld video game and asked, "So Julia, did they give you my mojo yet?" *Mojo? Where did that come from?*

Invoking the "you are so stupid" tone that siblings refine, Julia explained they had drawn his blood, not given her his marrow.

When the doctor called with the results, roughly six months after Julia first became ill, we finally had good news. Jack was a perfect match. He had the mojo.

As I learned more about BMTs, I realized we'd hit the jackpot. Not all donors can find a match. It was an incredible stroke of luck. Outcomes with related donors are dramatically better than those with unmatched donors.

There was no debate about whether Jack would step forward. Julia's life was at risk and Jack's mojo could save her. Of course he would be his sister's donor.

Years later, Jack confessed he had silently worried the transplant would not work. But it did work; and in a selfless act, he became the superhero he'd always dreamed he would be.

Fear and Resolve

WHEN PATIENTS on medical dramas need a bone marrow transplant, they undergo the extensive therapy in less than sixty minutes. In real life, the process is quite involved. Before Julia could have the transplant, both kids had to undergo a grueling battery of tests to evaluate whether Jack was healthy enough to be the donor and Julia able to handle the transplant.

The testing completed, Ted and I sat through a tense meeting with physicians who reviewed frightening statistics and complications, as well as potential outcomes. We were shell-shocked when we left the meeting, relieved we'd made the decision to go forward with the transplant beforehand. Otherwise, we didn't know if we could have summoned the courage to do so.

Julia had a general idea of the risks and benefits, but didn't share our concerns about whether she would experience organ failure, become infertile, or contract a secondary cancer. She was worried about whether she could play hockey and return to school. And she was worried about something that had never occurred to me.

"If I get Jack's bone marrow, will I get his autism?"

Her question stumped me. Experts were still investigating why a growing number of people have autism. I didn't know if it was transferrable through bone marrow. Though the doctors assured us it was not, I was apprehensive.

Despite her concerns, Julia was resolute and seemingly fearless.

"I'm having the transplant."

●

Ted and I were terrified. We spent nights thrashing about, battling fears of losing the bright, athletic, independent child whose kindergarten teacher had said, "Julia has the whole package."

I had to turn off my brain, lest it paralyze me. My friend Cynthia offered an invaluable gift. Whenever her mind takes off like a runaway train, she said, she visualizes a stop sign. She uses it to fend off worries and negative thoughts. The stop sign went into my growing toolkit for dealing with seemingly endless curve balls.

With minimal family support at hand and Ted busier than ever with his law practice, I worried about how I would care for a seriously ill child and a special needs teenager. I hired help for Jack and shifted my focus to Julia. Friends pitched in. Caitie and Dan came home from Denver and Chicago to celebrate the Easter holiday and the pre-transplant weekend.

I hired a photographer, fearing it might be our last opportunity to take a picture of our intact family. We spent a couple of hours at a picturesque spot on the Mississippi River, known as The Monument, with the photographer clicking away. Ironically, it was the same spot where Ted had suffered his heart attack less than seven years earlier.

As we were wrapping up the photo shoot, the photographer suggested we take a candid shot. Without hesitation, Ted and the kids crossed their eyes and arms and struck silly poses. I crossed my arms, stuck out my hip and looked at the camera, thinking, *Seriously*?

But it was a great idea, and the photo turned out to be a favorite—as well as the last one of the entire family together. Hiring the photographer was a prescient move—but not for the reason I'd imagined.

I Hate You, You Buttheads

JULIA'S TEACHERS and classmates were confused by what was about to occur. Before she entered the hospital, we crafted an explanation for her fifth grade classmates. Reading our note ten years later, it strikes me that, despite her bravery and maturity, Julia was still a little girl. After all, her email address was hoppinghappyfrogs @yahoo.com! I also realize how wrong we were about the 100 days, for it took far longer for her to get back into her hockey skates.

Titled "What's Up with Sully?" her message read:

Friday is my last day at school before I go to the hospital. As you know, I have a rare blood disorder called PNH. The only known cure for PNH is a bone marrow transplant (BMT). During spring break I am going into the hospital as an outpatient everyday to get tests and x-rays taken. On March 28 I am going to be admitted to the hospital. That week I am going to get my chemotherapy.

On April 5th I am getting the BMT. The BMT is not a surgery or an operation. I will have a tube put in me called a Hickman catheter, but I call it my hippo. They will take my brother's bone marrow out of him with a needle and put it in my hippo. After that I will be in the hospital for a few weeks or a month, depending on how well I do. After that, I am going to recover at home. It may take up to 100 days for a full recovery.

During that time I will have a website. It is www.caring-bridge.org/mn/sully. The website has a guestbook. You can click on the website and send me a note. I will also keep a journal of how I am doing. You can email me at hopping-happyfrogs@yahoo.com and you can instant message me at hockeyidiot911. I might be really bored, so let's stay in touch.

On the last Monday in March 2005, Ted, Julia, and I packed up the car with a large assortment of things Julia wanted to take along. We were wary, but optimistic.

When we stepped off the elevator, we began what felt like a death march across the hospital floor, arms overflowing with young girl stuff. There were few signs of life; it was hard to believe children dwelled behind the closed doors. As a nurse escorted us into our shoebox-sized room, Julia unleashed a piercing scream. In a desperate revolt, our eleven-year-old hurled fear and anger at her dad and me.

"You buttheads. I hate you! Take me home!"

The more she vented, the more Ted tried to reason her out of her rage. I sat stunned and silent, relieved she was finally reacting to the events of the previous nine months.

Our exhaustive journey had ended at the world-renowned bone marrow transplant center at the University of Minnesota Children's Hospital, thirty minutes from home. Throughout the months we'd spent in and out of medical offices with professionals inquiring, poking, and drawing blood, I hadn't seen Julia shed a tear. She was, indeed, her mother's daughter.

Her breakdown over, she became her resilient and creative self once again. She transformed her "prison cell" into her temporary home, finding places for her stuffed animals, funky hats, twinkling lights, and photos. Her tears dried up, returning sporadically over the months that followed.

The die was cast. "Sully's" fate was now in the hands of strangers.

The Magic Mojo

AS JULIA EXPLAINED to her friends, the first step was to prepare her body to accept Jack's bone marrow. Following a well-designed schedule, she went through a series of steps that were anguishing to witness. She was given chemotherapy and other powerful drugs that wreaked havoc on her stomach as they obliterated her immune system. As I watched in horror, technicians strapped my fragile daughter to a board to give her a single dose of full-body radiation.

With the medicine coursing through her bloodstream, the girl who could talk others into a coma seemed to slip into one herself. After months of actively pursuing a diagnosis, I sat helplessly as hours became days, fear my unyielding antagonist.

On transplant day, Ted and Jack arrived at the hospital early. Jack was sedated as his "mojo" was extracted from his hip with a large needle. His job done, he settled into a room across the hall from his sister, where he spent a few hours resting, raising and lowering the bed, and watching TV.

Late in the afternoon a nurse discharged him and gave him a T-shirt. He glanced at the gift and groused, "All I get is a T-shirt?"

Apparently, Jack had a bigger vision of what his gift would yield. He had become accustomed to a reward system early in life. Desperate to train him, I bought him a new toy every time he used the toilet. Consequently, he ended up with a huge collection of action figures. Understandably, with his sister's life at stake, he anticipated something more significant than a T-shirt.

The transplant was not the surgery many imagine. Nurses, encased in head-to-toe protective gear, attached a bag containing Jack's marrow to Julia's IV. What we prayed would be a magic potion silently dripped through the line, infiltrating her fragile system. In less than an hour, the transplant was underway.

The process felt anticlimactic until Julia's blood pressure spiked dramatically, prompting a frightening flurry of activity by doctors and nurses intent on stabilizing it. Though the journey was just beginning, we were already emotionally spent.

Knowing I hadn't lost my hair from my low-dose chemo, Julia refused to believe she would lose hers, despite many guarantees from doctors and nurses to the contrary. Watchful days passed before I saw a loose strand of dark, straight hair on her white pillowcase. It pained me to break the news.

Rather than wait for the hair to drop off at its own pace, I procured a razor from one of the nurses. Huddled next to her in the hospital shower, I shaved Julia's head as tears rolled down our cheeks.

All Over But the Waiting

WITH THE CHEMO, radiation, and mojo working out of sight, our focus shifted. It became a numbers game. Each day before sunrise, a technician drew blood while Julia slept. A few hours later a nurse wrote her blood counts on the white board across from the bed. Day after day we waited to learn whether her body had accepted Jack's marrow and was producing new blood cells. When her counts reached a certain level, she could go home.

Parents had minimal interaction with each other on the transplant floor. We were all there for one purpose, and it didn't involve socializing. One day when Julia was doing particularly well, I left her room to grab a coffee. A parent I'd never met joined me on the elevator. To fill the awkward moment, I uttered words I soon regretted.

"It's all over but the waiting now."

The weary stranger responded with silence.

That night, a family gathered in the visiting room located next to Julia's room for what proved to be a vigil. When we awoke the next morning, I saw an empty room down the hall. It belonged to the boy whose father I'd met on the elevator the previous day. The man, I realized with horror, had been waiting for a far different outcome than the one I anticipated for Julia.

Frantic, I implored one of the staff to tell me what had happened. Despite my pleas, she refused, citing patient confidentiality. The statistics from the intense implied consent meeting Ted and I had endured suddenly took shape. The way I understood the odds, only nine of fourteen patients would leave the floor with heartbeats. So this was how it worked. One day a child was there; the next he was gone.

The experience haunts me to this day.

Weapon of Mass Destruction

WE WERE EXCEEDINGLY LUCKY that Julia didn't experience any of the complications we'd been warned about, such as graft versus host disease (when the patient rejects the donor's marrow and develops various complications). Our biggest challenge was keeping her spirits up.

Ted and I took turns sleeping in her room on an inflatable mattress. We coaxed her to eat the hospital food she deemed "a weapon of mass destruction." We safeguarded her defenseless system against germs by limiting her visitors. As the days dragged on, our independent child became clingy. On the rare occasions I left the room while she was sleeping, I'd get a call if she woke up, her sleepy voice asking, "Where are you, Mom?

With little to occupy our time, we spent her waking hours watching TV or writing on her CaringBridge page. By day, we brown-eyed girls watched *Gilmore Girls*, a drama about a mother/daughter duo whose bond mirrored the one we were developing. At night we welcomed the humor of *Whose Line is it Anyway?*

Julia missed her friends, but she really missed her dog Sara. Throughout her hospital stay, Julia begged us to bring our Cavalier King Charles spaniel for a visit. I wracked my brain for ways to connect patient with puppy, but it simply wasn't feasible. Julia was on an isolation floor; rigorous protocols ensured patients were not exposed to anything that could imperil their health.

Ted did his best to add levity to a humorless situation. When he stayed overnight at the hospital, he always packed his good humor. If Dr. Margy MacMillan entered the room, he'd greet her with a standard question, "Hey doc, when do we get that steak sandwich and Sam Adams beer?" On occasion, he also packed a bottle of wine in his duffel bag. When Margy heard about the wine, she busted Ted for breaking the rules.

With her infectious laugh, Margy put us at ease, making jokes and playing with Julia's toys, but cautioning us she was only being so jocular because Julia was doing well. So well, in fact, that less than a month after she branded us "buttheads," Julia was discharged to outpatient care. It was near record time for a transplant patient at the University of Minnesota Children's Hospital. Many patients spend months in the hospital, waiting for new marrow or fighting the complications Julia had been lucky to dodge.

We checked out of the hospital on a day when the sun shone so brightly it burned my eyes. Julia left with a bandana covering her bare head and a paper mask covering her mouth. With Ted in Estonia on business, I left with palpitations. The stellar, 24/7 care had ended, and I was now primary caregiver of our medically fragile child.

Running in Circles

WE LEARNED that Julia qualified for a wish from the Make-a-Wish Foundation. The organization arranges a wide range of experiences for children with life-threatening illnesses. It sends patients and their families on getaways to Disneyland and Hawaii; arranges for kids to swim with dolphins and meet their favorite athletes or musicians.

Julia chose none of the options that involved adventure or relaxation. Instead, to the dismay of our family, she asked for another dog. She wanted Sara to have a companion. Though we tried to subtly steer her in a different direction, we could only push so hard. Julia was the patient, and it was her wish.

Friends and family thought I was crazy to entertain the idea of bringing another dog into our home. Kids always make unfulfilled promises to parents that we accept with a wink and a nod: If you get me a dog, I will take care of it. Julia wasn't able to take care of a dog and made no bones about it. Without question, another dog would generate more work for me.

I was exhausted and scared. I couldn't fathom assuming responsibility for another living being. But Julia had gone to a dark, unrecognizable place. She was lonely and often in great pain, her bones aching from her medication. I didn't know this unhappy child. My daughter was a high energy, blow-the-socks-off-of-everyday gal. Digging deep into an almost empty cauldron of energy, I capitulated—with one condition. We would get another dog . . . but it had to be housebroken.

●

We found Dylan on the Internet. He was ten months old and lived close to our home. Like Sara, he was an adorable Blenheim Cavalier King Charles spaniel. Though Julia's wish was granted, life with Dylan was not a dream-come-true. Soon after we brought him home, we discovered he wasn't housebroken. He didn't answer to his name. And he had a bizarre habit of chasing his ears until he would catch one in his mouth. He ran in circles. Ten minutes. Twenty minutes. Thirty minutes. Worse yet, he was a neurotic barker. The combination taxed my frazzled nerves.

We might have been able to tolerate Dylan's eccentric habits, for he was cute and sweet, and both Julia and Sara loved having another dog in the house. But when he began to run out of the yard, up the steep hill behind our house, and onto the busy road behind it, my family reached a tacit understanding. We were living with enough fear. Death had been lurking in the wings for too long. Dylan had to go before something tragic happened.

I Miss My Life

IT WAS A LONG SUMMER: quieter, with just one dog.

"I miss my life," Julia, once such a social butterfly, said.

I missed mine, too. I'd been consumed by autism and illnesses for so long I scarcely recalled anything else. The relentless crises were besting me. I often felt like a boxer being pummeled in the ring. Jab. Cross. Hook. Uppercut.

As we watched curly hair sprout on Julia's head, I scurried about, trying to feed, amuse, and comfort her during days that passed so slowly it seemed the sand had stalled in the hourglass.

Jack often got short shrift as his little sister's needs taxed my dwindling energy. Ted and I had little time alone. But there was an unspoken understanding between us. We could have spent much more time in the hospital . . . or lost our child, like other parents we'd met.

Though one rationale for Julia's transplant was to avoid transfusions, it took months for her body to accept Jack's bone marrow and begin to produce its own blood cells. While we waited for the pokey bone marrow to produce the necessary blood cells, Julia returned to the outpatient clinic for more than forty red blood cell transfusions.

In a follow-up visit years later, we learned the iron level in her blood was so high from all the transfusions she was at risk for heart and lung problems. So we added phlebotomy to her long list of medical procedures. She returned to the clinic numerous times to be hooked up to an IV and have her red blood cells *removed*!

Eventually, Julia's energy, appetite, and weight returned; and the black circles under her eyes disappeared. She grudgingly accepted her hair would be curly instead of straight.

As the beginning of the school year approached, she became insistent about rejoining her classmates, now sixth graders. I feared germs would lead to fevers and a mandatory hospitalization, for there was a narrow margin between health and danger for Julia. If she spiked a temperature of 100.3, we were to take her directly to the emergency room so she could be admitted to the hospital. We'd been there once; I dreaded a recurrence.

I reluctantly arranged for her to return to school. I met with her teachers and explained that her immune system was still fragile and she tired easily. Off she went.

In November, I read on CaringBridge that another girl who had a transplant about the same time as Julia had returned to school, contracted pneumonia, and died. My fear was another family's reality. I freaked and pulled my daughter from school.

Julia returned in January to teachers who questioned what she did when she was absent, not comprehending how vulnerable she was to illness. One teacher welcomed her back by directing her to sit in the common area and catch up on homework while her classmates enjoyed a class party.

I was livid.

In the fall of 2006, we enrolled Julia at a small all-girls Catholic school close to home. The welcoming and nurturing environment we found at the Convent of the Visitation was quite a contrast to her previous school. The faculty and administrators were accommodating and understanding throughout her six-year tenure as a Vis girl.

Although the PNH was gone, Julia's new immune system never returned to par. Throughout middle and high school, she missed hundreds of classes due to frequent illnesses. She sustained two concussions, playing hockey and soccer, and missed even more school. Yet she excelled in her classes, played sports, and enjoyed an active social life.

Eventually, I stopped waiting for another shoe to drop. Life was going well until midway through her sophomore year, when another shoe *did* drop—just not the one I feared.

part
three

*A Heart
Too Big*

You Didn't Need to Ask Me

DECEMBER 2009 will forever serve as a reminder of how much life can change in a heartbeat. I was honing my skills as a columnist for the St. Paul *Pioneer Press*. Caitie was living in Denver with her boyfriend Peter, establishing a reputation in the public relations arena. Dan was living in Virginia with his girlfriend Nicole, but was itching to move. They'd had their fill of the Washington, DC, political scene in which they worked.

Jack was making strides at his boarding school in New Hampshire. Julia was having a rough fall as a sophomore at Visitation. Though the bone marrow transplant had cured her of PNH, her immune system was still fragile. She'd suffered through mono and pneumonia in quick succession and was sick and tired of being sick and tired.

Ted was busy practicing law. He was proud to say he'd educated his older kids well and they had landed jobs with benefits. His work was done. He was eager to share adult life with them and was hoping to entice Dan to return to Minnesota.

The second weekend in December I flew to Maryland to meet my brother Steve's newborn, Isabel. I planned to spend a few days helping with the baby, and then return to Minnesota in time for Ted to fly to Boston. He was going to meet with colleagues before bringing Jack home from boarding school for the holiday break.

At noon on Tuesday, December 15, I called Ted at the law firm he'd started with his partners shortly before Jack was born in 1991.

I was holding Isabel, inhaling that sweet, fresh-from-the-bath baby scent. With no forethought, I blurted out a question.

"I love this baby girl," I said, nuzzling the folds in her neck. "Could I tell Steve and Shari we would be their guardians if, God forbid, anything happened to them?"

"Absolutely," Ted replied, with no hesitation. "You didn't need to ask me that."

"Of course I needed to ask you. It was the respectful thing to do. But I knew what your answer would be."

With a quick exchange of "I love you," we ended our last conversation.

What's Going On?

THAT NIGHT Steve, Shari, Isabel, and I went to dinner with Steve's oldest son, Mark. As we returned to their home, I noticed I had missed calls on my cellphone. Seated in the car, I learned from Julia that a doctor had called from the hospital Ted had visited so many times. He'd told her nothing except that her dad was in the emergency room. She'd explained that I was away and she was home alone, unable to drive because she was months shy of obtaining her drivers license.

Though I knew Ted was in the emergency room, my conversation with the doctor came as a complete shock: Ted had suffered a heart attack while driving home from the health club . . . an ambulance had transported him to the hospital . . . they had done everything they could . . . but he was sorry to say . . . . We'd need to identify a funeral home, the doctor continued, but given I was 1,200 miles from home, I could address that detail in due course.

Over time, the story came together like a jigsaw puzzle, with pieces gathered from Ted's cellphone, and the people who'd spoken to him in the final hours of his life. Ted had dropped Julia at hockey practice in St. Paul before he went to the nearby health club. A friend drove Julia home from the rink because Ted had promised to meet his friend John McDonald for dinner in Minneapolis.

Ted was heading away from Minneapolis when he pulled over, called 911, and took his nitroglycerine. His cellphone revealed he'd spent several minutes on the phone with the dispatcher before the

60

ambulance arrived. Whether he'd appreciated the gravity of his condition is unknown; but I suspect he did, for he rarely took the nitroglycerine and wasn't prone to calling 911.

Much of what transpired after my conversation with the emergency room physician remains a blur. I recall bits and pieces of painful conversations, particularly with Julia, who called while I was trying to organize my thoughts and make a plan.

"WHAT'S GOING ON? The nurse from the hospital just called and asked what funeral home they should send Dad's body to," my tough-as-nails girl screamed into the phone.

I took a deep breath, asked her what she knew, and then filled in the gaps.

When she'd calmed down, I hung up, called the hospital, and asked for the nurse who had shattered my daughter's world. I screamed and swore at her until I was hoarse.

"Do you realize that for the rest of her life my daughter is going to remember how she learned her father died? How could you do that?"

After I composed myself, I made more calls than I can recount: to Caitie in Denver, Dan in Virginia, Ted's brother and law partners in Minneapolis, his best friends in Florida and Illinois, and my closest friends at home.

I prefaced the conversations with "Are you sitting down?"

Caitie and Ted's brother Tom were sitting—in their cars. I tried to stall Caitie until she had arrived home, but she sensed something was wrong and pried the words from my lips, responding with an anguished cry.

Tom, the closest of Ted's four brothers, had just pulled into his driveway with his sons. His initial disbelief yielded to action. The youngest of seven, Tom stepped up in a big way for our family, going alone to the hospital to identify Ted's body and collect his personal belongings. Then he retrieved our car—still parked on a St. Paul street with the driver's seat reclined.

We got word to every family member except eighteen-year-old

Jack, who was away at school. I had no idea how my sensitive son would react to the death of the man he adored.

My mind flashed on the time Ted took Jack and Dan to a Broadway show in New York. Afterward, he let Jack run around Times Square, hands flapping (stimming), as many people with autism are wont to do. Ted assured me no one would raise an eyebrow to Jack's behavior in the bustling melting pot of New York. How many dads would roll that way? I knew I had to break the news to Jack in person.

My phone rang again. The unfamiliar voice belonged to a woman from LifeSource. She was calling to initiate the organ donation process. Of course, Ted had checked the box. I had limited time to answer what felt like an exhaustive list of personal questions. It was such a grueling process I wondered whether it was worth the effort. Weeks later, I received a letter reporting Ted's bone and tissue were gifted to eighty-four people, aged fifteen to eighty-two, in seventeen states. It was the final act of a generous man. I was glad I'd endured the process.

The moment he heard the news, my brother Steve went right to work. As I was fielding phone calls in his kitchen, he was booking a flight to Minnesota.

Hours later I was lying in the darkness in Steve's basement bedroom when my phone rang. It was Caitie, calling in the wee hours of the night to check in with me.

"Are we still going to be a family?" I asked.

She assured me we were.

After a sleepless night, I packed my suitcase and prepared for the dreaded trip home. Leaving my exhausted sister-in-law with their five-week-old baby, Steve drove to the airport and shepherded me onto the plane. Tears streamed down our faces for much of the flight, as we silently entertained our respective thoughts.

●

Toilet Paper, Flowers, and Hugs

THE NEWS OF TED'S DEATH spread quickly in our community of 10,000. It wasn't yet noon when Steve and I walked into my house, filled with friends with stricken faces. They'd arrived with food, toilet paper, flowers, beverages, tears, and hugs.

I found Julia downstairs on our sectional surrounded by her classmates, young schoolgirls in blue uniform skirts and white blouses who had lost their innocence when they learned the popular Mr. Sullivan was gone.

From the moment I stepped into the house, I was overwhelmed by a whirlwind of activity and difficult decisions. At some point, my doorbell rang, and I greeted a friend I hadn't seen in ages. I'd met Sondra when our girls were preschool classmates a decade earlier. She was standing in my threshold with a plate of cookies and a question.

"Do you need anything?"

I was beginning to grasp how much needed to be done. I studied Sondra's face and asked her if she was serious. She insisted she was.

"I need to have Jack's sport coat dry cleaned for the funeral."

"I'm on it," she said. A day later, Jack's blue blazer was hanging on my front door knob, encased in dry cleaner's plastic.

I was moved and grateful that Sondra had reached out to help. I sensed she was also grateful to have a chance to do something, anything, to help. I learned an important lesson in that brief encounter with one of many angels in my life.

It is as much a gift to accept an offer of help as it is to extend one.

*

Where's Dad?

THE OLDER KIDS had planned to come home for Christmas. Ted's death rushed their return. Caitie flew home with Peter. Dan and Nicole drove from Virginia with their dog Buckley.

One of us, typically Ted, escorted Jack back and forth to boarding school, flying to Boston, renting a car for the two-hour drive to campus, then turning around to repeat the trip home. With Ted gone, we needed another plan.

His brother Tom stepped up again. We arranged for Jack to meet his uncle at the Boston airport. The round trip made for a long day for Tom, but it was the easiest way to bring Jack home.

Not knowing whether Jack would ask why Uncle Tom was there instead of his dad, much less how he would react to the news, I was wound so tight I feared I would snap. I paced and worried; would Jack fall apart? If he did, could I summon the strength to put him back together? I was dangling by a thread, but I was a seasoned survivor of crises. Jack was not. Moreover, Ted was his best—his only—friend, as well as the one who was supposed to teach him how to be a man.

While we waited for Jack and Tom to return, other family members arrived. The female contingent—Caitie, Julia, Traci, and Ted's sister Therese—focused our tired brains on the details of putting a person to rest.

We engaged in a spirited discussion about burial versus cremation. A passionate Green Bay Packers fan, Ted had said more than once that he wanted his ashes spread at Lambeau Field. Was he serious, or was that just another of his endless jokes? Some thought he was serious (at least about the cremation). Others could not abide the notion of fire. Ultimately, was it more important to honor what we thought he wanted, or to choose an option we could live with?

We settled on burying him at a cemetery close to our home. The decision made, I purchased plots for the two of us and for Jack, determining that while his siblings would likely have families of their own, Jack and I were paired for life. Most importantly, I wanted to avoid a repeat of the grueling conversation after I died.

Most of the family had gathered by the time the guys returned from New Hampshire. Jack hadn't asked why Tom was there instead of Ted. He was just happy to leave school a few days early. He walked into the kitchen and greeted Dan and Nicole, Caitie and Peter, his aunts and uncle with a big smile.

Then he surveyed the room and asked, "Where's Dad?"

I steered him to the sofa and sat next to him as the others gathered around. Our dog Sara followed, nesting at our feet.

I began the conversation by reminding Jack of Ted's health history. He cut to the chase. "So he's dead?"

Memories vary on what happened next. I recall silence; Julia recalls Jack unleashing a tearless cry reminiscent of an animal's wail. We all agree that he looked down at our eight-year-old dog before uttering unexpected words.

"No offense, Sara, but I thought you'd die first."

A few moments passed before he excused himself to play video games.

The next morning Jack caught me off guard once again. As I plied my sleepless body with caffeine, he cruised into the kitchen with two questions on his mind.

"Mom, are we financially sound?"

"Are you going to remarry?"

I fumbled with an answer he apparently deemed satisfactory, because he left the kitchen as quickly as he had entered it.

But my son had hit a nerve. I managed the daily finances and Ted handled the long-term planning. We never got around to having the financial summit that would have been prudent. It took some time before I knew the answer to Jack's question.

The funeral was beautiful, the effort of many hearts and hands. I realized later how little I knew about anything that happened outside my bubble of grief. Word had somehow spread to the right people. Many traveled to Minnesota at a very inconvenient time to pay their respects.

Friends arranged the funeral luncheon, along with Ted's sister Therese. Father James Lies celebrated the funeral mass at St. Peter's Church. When "Ave Maria," was sung, as it had been at our wedding, I felt as though some sort of circle was complete—till death do us part.

When Tom spoke on that cold December day, he reminded the gatherers of one of Ted's favorite sayings: "There's no such thing as bad weather; there's just bad gear."

As I glanced over at Jack, I wondered how he would weather this unexpected storm, particularly when he returned to school in New Hampshire.

Second-Guessing and Speculation

I REMEMBER LITTLE about that Christmas, other than my friends, Peg and Brian, arriving with a gift. They were concerned there would be nothing for me under the tree. Ted, a Christmas Eve shopper, had insisted on buying gifts that year. The kids knew he'd purchased a few things. I had found cameras and a computer hidden in a drawer. I cobbled together other gifts, many personal items of Ted's I thought the kids might treasure as keepsakes.

The holidays passed with an abundance of emotions—sadness, disbelief, anxiety, anger, and gratitude. The older kids flew back to Virginia and Denver. When school resumed, Julia returned to Visitation and Jack to New Hampshire with his uncle escorting him once again.

I'd been so exhausted I was afraid to drive anywhere, lest I have an accident and render my children orphans. But my resolve matched my exhaustion. If anything happened to me, I wanted a plan to be in place. I rewrote my will and established a special needs trust for Jack.

I suppose it's inevitable with a sudden death. Survivors speculate; we search in the rear view mirror for hints or signs of what was to come. There were several moments that picked away at my consciousness, causing me to wonder whether Ted had any inkling that his heart was as fragile as it turned out to be.

In late September, we had spent a few days with two of our favorite couples, John and Sonya, and Matt and Maggie, in Ashville,

North Carolina. Though Ted was suffering from a foot injury, he insisted on accompanying us on a hike. His stamina was poor, he was red-faced and he struggled to keep up. As he lingered behind, the rest of us exchanged worried glances. Though we sensed he was dealing with more than a bad foot, no one verbalized our concerns.

The following month, Ted and I were poised to visit Jack in New Hampshire for a biannual parents' weekend. Early in the week, Ted felt pressure in his chest, so he went to the hospital for a stress test. I waited nervously for the results, fearing he would be hospitalized. I dreaded the possibility of having to choose between staying with him and traveling to New Hampshire without him. Jack missed us terribly. He anxiously anticipated the weekend visits, and ended every letter home with "I hope to see you."

I never met with the cardiologist after the stress test. The doctor apparently said Ted didn't need an angioplasty that day, but that he would require bypass surgery *some day*. Ted brushed off talk of surgery; he couldn't take that much time off of work.

Less than two months later, Ted pulled off the road and called 911. The man who loved cars took his last ride in an ambulance with strangers who barely got him to the emergency room before his heart failed.

Second-guessing and speculation often visited in the unbearable quiet of the night. I began leaving the television on when I went to bed. Its incessant prattle filled the palpable emptiness in our bedroom. Though Ted had traveled frequently, I felt his absence differently now. Thoughts that he would return, drop his suitcase on the floor, and fill the room with his energy gradually evaporated.

Day by day, the numbness chipped away, like an artist honing an ice sculpture. I began to think of grief as a wave. I imagined myself standing at the edge of the ocean, knowing the waves would roll in, but never knowing how gentle or fierce they would be. At times, small waves would graze my ankles. Other times, menacing waves would knock me over like the pins on a bowling lane. I would pull myself up and brace for the next wave, never knowing if it would stroke my ankles or buckle my knees.

Legacy

BY SPRINGTIME, I'd confirmed Ted had taken steps to provide well for the kids and me. His life insurance, retirement, and ownership interest in the law firm ensured we could remain in our family home and continue the kids' education. I had the luxury of figuring out what my next steps would be, without the pressure of re-entering a workforce that had changed dramatically since my departure twenty years earlier.

I continued to receive cards and messages from people who had known Ted. As gratified as I was to learn that Ted had touched so many people, I was distressed that he would never know how they felt. He'd often said that he didn't feel appreciated. Other than his high school buddies, he felt he had few close friends.

I wished he could have known that hundreds gathered to celebrate his life and mourn his passing; that cards and emails poured in from people I knew well and people I'd never met, but who felt they knew me because Ted talked so often about his family. I wished he could have known that our neighbor Matthew dedicated his Eagle Scout award to him. I wished he could have known that teenagers, law partners, neighbors, and professional adversaries would share so many sentiments and memories, all of which confirmed he was a man who mattered to many.

I wish he knew that he left an enviable legacy, reflected in the notes and cards I read through my tears.

"He didn't teach us how to live; he lived and let us watch him do it."

"He was the most generous man anyone could have met. He always put himself last, and his friends and family first. He also was more hip than anyone I knew. He wore a flat-brimmed Yankees hat backwards and he was the only person I know who could do that."

"The most charismatic and loving man that I have ever met. Everyone will truly miss 'Big Ted,' the man who had too big of a heart."

The nurse who had called Julia shortly after Ted died sent a heartfelt note. "I had cared for Mr. Sullivan as a patient before that fateful night and remembered him immediately because of his sense of humor and kindness. Unfortunately, the last time we met, I couldn't help him enough, and my conversation with your daughter only made bad, worse. I am so terribly sorry . . . ."

Unfortunately she didn't provide a return address; I wanted her to know I accepted her apology.

I learned more about Ted's final day at work from a law partner who described Ted as the heart and soul of the firm.

"On the 15th, Ted held court in his office to share some well-worn pearls of wisdom with associates. Some pearls were new—gained from more recent experiences in his life. Some I had heard from the days when I started. One thing he stressed to all associates and his partners . . . was that he felt like the luckiest and most fortunate man on earth. And he wanted us to feel that way, too."

As I plodded through exhausting days and sleepless nights, one thought sustained me. In any relationship, particularly marriage, we have many conversations. Inevitably, some will involve harsh words and intense emotions. Like grief, marriage has crashing waves, soothing waves, and an undertow.

Despite persistent stress and challenges, Ted and I had resisted the undertow, though we'd certainly had our share of crashing waves. A couple of weeks before he died, we'd had a heated argument.

Though we hadn't resolved our disagreement, we'd moved on, as we were prone to do. I've taken great solace in knowing our last conversation was a soothing wave; we'd made a pact to be Isabel's guardian— to support people we loved, with no consideration for how it might affect us. That was who we were as individuals, and as a couple.

Déjà Vu

THE LAST WEEKEND in February 2010 was parents' weekend at Jack's boarding school. Dan flew up from Virginia so I wouldn't have to go alone. He was eager to see Jack's school and to spend time with his younger brother. I welcomed his company. It was a good, but melancholy, weekend for all of us.

When I landed in Minneapolis late on Sunday, I turned on my phone and read a text from my friend Lisa: our neighbor, John Mc-Donald, had just died of a heart attack. *What?*

I exited the plane in a daze. I looked up to see my daughter Julia standing with her friend Claire and Claire's mom, Kelly. The two girls had arrived at the Minneapolis airport shortly before me. They'd spent the weekend in Denver with Caitie, celebrating Julia's sixteenth birthday.

As we left the gate together, I was overcome by a new wave of familiar emotions. We were still processing Ted's death. It was inconceivable that our long-time friend and neighbor had collapsed next to his treadmill. We were well aware of Ted's condition. Though John's father had died of a heart attack, he'd had no warning that he would suffer the same fate.

John had spent a fun-filled weekend at Creighton University with his daughter Ellie and several other fathers and daughters. Now Ellie and Julia, friends since birth, were fatherless. It was unfathomable.

John's wife Ann had been my steadfast companion since Ted's death. Like many of my friends, she'd worried about joining the

·

73

freakin' widows club. Yet, she was utterly unprepared to lose her charismatic husband, a trial lawyer with whom I'd briefly practiced in the infancy of my career.

It was a stunning blow for the McDonalds and their extensive network of family and friends. It was a crushing shock for Julia, who had looked forward to obtaining her driver's license the next day and experiencing a bit of adolescent joy during our time of mourning. My heart ached for everyone. As I looked at Julia, I realized that, for the rest of her life, her birthday would be marked by the joy of life and the memory of death.

Bitter or Better

BEFORE JULIA underwent her bone marrow transplant, I occasionally allowed myself to contemplate the worst—that she would not survive and that we would need to plan her funeral. Were that to happen, I wanted to be able to turn to a familiar church.

I am a person of faith, but I haven't found my home. I've often felt like I have one foot in the Catholic Church. I was baptized and made my First Communion shortly before I was yanked away from my Catholic father, so I never went through Confirmation. I've been divorced; I married a man who was divorced.

I tend to be rule-bound. I struggle with many of the church "rules," ranging from taking communion to using birth control. I'm horrified by the documented claims of pedophilia. If I don't subscribe to all the rules, how do I participate legitimately? Ted didn't follow all the church rules, either, but that caused him no angst. He was born a Catholic. He would die a Catholic. Moreover, he lived by the mantra that rules were advisory for Sullivans.

Over the years, we belonged to a couple of Catholic churches in our area but had never become committed parishioners. But it was important to him that the kids get a Catholic education. Though Jack attended public school so he could receive special education services, Julia, Dan, and Caitie attended parochial schools.

It's interesting to me that one of my most powerful life lessons came from a Catholic priest with whom I shared a few moments in a darkened room. I'm not sure I would recognize him if I saw him again, but I will never forget his words.

In April 2010, Ann and I dressed up and headed to the high school where our boys had become young men, and where many friends awaited. St. Thomas Academy was holding its annual fundraising dinner and auction, and Peg and Brian Reagan had invited us to be their guests.

A few hours (and a couple glasses of wine) into the evening, I met Father Joseph Johnson. We exchanged pleasantries; then I unloaded my grief onto the kind priest who was just enjoying his Saturday night.

I told him about the people who had rallied on my family's behalf early on—the hundreds of family members, friends, neighbors, classmates, and colleagues who attended Ted's funeral on a bitterly cold Saturday morning, just days before the students had final exams and only a week before Christmas.

I told him how helpful some family members and friends had been, arranging the funeral luncheon, taking my car to be washed before the funeral, sweeping out my garage, hanging Christmas lights, and walking my dog.

I told him about the wing men—my sister Traci, who was by my side at the exhausting, four-hour wake that drew judges, politicians, and friends from around the country; and my high school friend Pat, who took Jack home when he refused to attend the burial because cemeteries creeped him out.

I told him about Julia's classmates who, at the conclusion of the funeral mass, stood in formation in their blue uniforms and white gloves, tears streaming down dozens of cheeks, as my family followed Ted's casket to the hearse where the bagpiper played in the bitter cold.

I told him about the bolters; the people I'd expected to be present but who had vanished, become silent, or worse yet, uncooperative, as I tended to the children's needs, sorted through piles of paperwork, and addressed financial tasks.

I told him about the widower who not only called Ted a spendthrift because he had sent his children to private schools, but also suggested I would drink myself to sleep every night, as he had after his wife died.

Finally, I shared that seventy-six days after Ted's heart failed, our friend John suffered the same fate, rendering his wife, Ann, my sister in grief. I asked him why two men who lit up the room with engaging personalities had died in their mid-fifties, while people who'd been selfish and cruel and led unhealthy lives were still alive and probably would be for years.

My weary eyes pleaded for answers. He had none. Instead, he offered words that set the course for my future.

"I can't explain why Ted and John died, or why these things happened to you when you have already experienced so much adversity in your life. But I can tell you that when faced with difficult situations, we all have a choice.

We can be bitter.

Or we can be better."

I put Father Johnson's words in my hip pocket. Bitter or better. They became my North Star.

part
four

*Autism—
From Angst to
Acceptance*

I Never Knew

I BEGAN WRITING in 2005 when Julia had her bone marrow transplant. Founded not far from my Minnesota home, CaringBridge is a nonprofit organization that offers an online platform so people dealing with medical situations, or other life crises, can connect with their supporters.

Initially, CaringBridge was a way for Julia to stay in touch with her friends. Family and friends sent messages and jokes. I generally posted updates on her progress. Eventually, she lost interest, but I spent many quiet moments reading and writing, first in the hushed hospital room, later at home.

We'd met other fellow travelers at the University of Minnesota Children's Hospital, most from other parts of the country. They understood our journey, for it was their journey, too.

I watched other women in this new sorority deal with their heartache with grace and strength. Two young mothers buried their babies when their transplants failed.

Other families spent months in and out of the hospital, lives hanging by a thread. As difficult as our experience was, it was not as bad as what many others endured. Everything in life is relative. And we were blessed.

In the late summer of 2006, I responded to a call for submissions for an anthology titled *Special Gifts: Women Writers on the Heartache, the Happiness and the Hope of Raising a Special Needs Child*. I turned my attention to Jack and the challenges we'd faced for fifteen years. Hunched over my keyboard late into the night, years of grief seeped through my fingers as I recounted Jack's developmental and medical issues.

Days later, I had difficulty breathing. I went to the emergency room with which I was so familiar, fearful it was my turn to have a heart attack, but assured I was not. I had released a pressure valve that had been screwed on tight for years. Grief, I realized, will wait patiently if ignored, but eventually it will surface. While it seemed writing was my release—my outlet—there were too many memories and emotions to discharge in one sitting.

A year after the anthology was published, my in-laws, Tom and Marilyn, came for one of their infrequent visits. Marilyn asked to see the book. On an August afternoon, she sat on our back deck, turning the pages as she gained new insight into my family's life. After a bit, she stepped into the kitchen and handed the book back to me, eyes glistening. "I never knew," she said, voice full of regret. She wished they had lived closer so she could have been more helpful.

Jack had grown from a toddler to a teen before his grandmother fully appreciated what we had been dealing with since she shared her fear that he was deaf. Her reaction reminded me that parents are not the only ones who experience confusion, shattered dreams, and the need to revise their expectations when a professional labels unusual behavior and communication patterns.

Though we'd done our best to explain Jack's autism to family, it was an ongoing learning process for us, too. Grandma Marilyn was from a generation in which people with autism were hidden from view, often in institutions. The institutions have been shuttered and people like her grandson have become increasingly visible. They are working, recreating, traveling—living among the rest of us. Yet that does not mean they are understood or accepted—by grandparents or others.

The point was underscored one day when I was getting a pedicure. Two women sat an arm's length away, one painting the other's toes. The client had spent the holiday weekend with extended family members, including her eight-year-old nephew with autism.

"He would not listen and only ate pizza," she vented.

I bit my tongue as I realized her solution was to give the boy a good dose of discipline.

There was a time when I, too, would have jumped to judgment about a child who refuses to partake in the family meal, doesn't respond when spoken to, and spoils the family getaway. But Jack and his peers have helped me to view those behaviors through a different lens.

There are certainly children who should be disciplined when they throw tantrums to get their way. But for people with autism, family gatherings and time away from the familiarity and routine of home can generate stress at a level I still struggle to comprehend. What would be considered naughty, or antisocial behavior, for people without their challenges may likely be a sign of sensory overload or the inability to cope with change.

Temple Grandin is an internationally recognized author, speaker, and autism advocate. Through her speeches and books, the Colorado State University professor has not only given a voice to people on the autism spectrum, she has helped others to understand them better.

Temple says that, while challenges to the sensory system are common in people on the autism spectrum, they are not well understood. "If you receive the same sensory information as everyone else, but your brain interprets it differently, then your experience will be dramatically—even painfully—different from those around you."

She has encountered people whose hearing fades in and out, so that words go from sounding like a bad mobile phone connection to fireworks exploding. She has talked to kids who cannot tolerate the sound of the scoreboard buzzer in a gymnasium. Younger kids may throw a tantrum because they cannot handle the sensory overload but can't communicate their distress with words.

Too often, parents, already stressed by their children's challenging behaviors, are met with looks or comments from friends, family, and strangers who wrongly assume that lack of discipline is the root of a much more complex problem. The more family members understand about the child's need for routine and predictability, and sensory and communication challenges, the easier it will be to enjoy their time together.

Stillwater, Minnesota, author Sylvia Miller Grubb has a grandson named Micah who is about the same age as my son Jack. Sylvia and Micah's father, Stuart, wrote a book to help families navigate the kinds of problems the woman in the salon was complaining about.

In *Grandparenting a Child with Autism*, the authors explain that a child might throw a tantrum in the grocery store checkout line or refuse to eat his dinner because noises, lights, smells, and strangers cause too much stress. While the child may need discipline, he also may be experiencing anxiety and frustration about a change in routine or his inability to communicate.

Family members may also not understand why some children on the autism spectrum display odd speaking patterns (or do not speak at all), repeat random lines from favorite movies, or refer to themselves in the third person. Because some people on the spectrum can be very literal, they may misunderstand common idioms such as "beating around the bush." With greater insight, family members are less likely to impute poor parenting or bad manners to a child's failure to look them in the eye.

I'm grateful for insights from people like Temple and the Grubbs. Recognizing the value to me, I've joined the chorus of parents who share insights and perspective so others might be more receptive to, and compassionate toward, the growing population of Jacks, Temples, and Micahs.

Extraordinary Vigilance

WHEN I READ the essays in the anthology, I found the heartache was so pervasive I could only dip my toe into it. Judging from the writings, we mothers lived with some hope, but with little happiness. I had written about Jack and his autism on a whim, more to unburden my heart than to launch a new career. But that, apparently, was the plan.

On Jack's sixteenth birthday, as my family was driving through Wisconsin, I was reflecting on what, for most teens, is a landmark birthday. My heart was heavy. Birthdays are tough when your child does not march to the same drummer as his peers. Once they get beyond the age where every child in the class is invited to every party, kids like Jack often fall off the invitation list. It is no easier on his birthday. Who do you invite for cake and ice cream when your child has no friends? It is one of many situations in which a parent must discern whose heart is breaking—hers or her child's.

The radio interrupted my thoughts with a troubling news report. A young boy with autism was missing and a search was underway. Words began careening through my head as I thought about Jack and the missing toddler.

As soon as we got home I composed an essay that incorporated my disparate thoughts from that day. I sent it to Mike Burbach, the opinion page editor for the St. Paul *Pioneer Press* at the time. Within days, he had published the first of more than 150 submissions I've written since 2007 as a contributing columnist.

• • •

Driving through central Wisconsin, I battled the melancholy that crawls into my heart each year around the birth date of my first-born—my son, whose needs have driven me to near exhaustion and stretched the limits of my patience; my son, who is clever and sweet and has expanded my level of compassion; my son, who will likely never take a driving test. My son, who has autism.

In a freaky coincidence, a radio newscaster interrupted my reverie to announce that local authorities had found the body of seven-year-old Benjy Heil floating in a pond less than a mile from his Wisconsin home. Benjy had disappeared the week before from his family home—not for the first time. Scores of volunteers rallied to search for him.

My melancholy quickly became despair for the parents who received the news I feared hearing for so many years. My first thought was, *there but for the grace of God, go I.* My mind turned to the boy we called Jumping Jack Flash because he never stopped moving. Our curious wanderer who made unsupervised visits to our neighbors, rendering us breathless with panic; the boy for whom we ultimately installed a big black fence in our suburban backyard after neighbors called to report our toddler had entered their home unsupervised. I recalled those exhausting years when we were vigilantes: anticipating and preparing for unknown dangers always lurking in the background.

For many people, autism is a lifelong condition, although it manifests differently over time. Thousands of families will deal with autism-related issues for a lifetime: medical, behavioral, therapeutic, educational, vocational, and housing concerns. The disproportionate amount of time and energy devoted to the child with autism affects the siblings, the parents, and the extended family, and frequently results in painful social isolation.

Families often spend considerable sums to pursue every

conceivable treatment option for their child. But most of all, living with autism can require extraordinary vigilance where one must always know what the child is doing and stay one step ahead of him—a demand that is incomprehensible to most who don't shoulder it, and virtually impossible to achieve.

The Quest for Normalcy

AFTER THE FIRST ESSAY was published, I received a flurry of emails from readers who thanked me for telling their story. Again I found myself in a club with other women who shared my fears and heartache, strangers who also felt overwhelmed and isolated, who longed for someone to lift the curtain on the mystery surrounding their lives.

I recognized I had a receptive audience for my insights, matched by my reluctance to continue to focus on something that had thoroughly depleted me. I didn't want my future to be all about my past. Yet, few were writing about autism, and I had more to say. If my writing would encourage readers to be more compassionate toward my son—my family—and others who wore our shoes, then there was value in relinquishing some of my family's privacy and stepping into the spotlight.

For the second column, I rewound the clock and started from the beginning of our story.

. . .

I can't recall the person who first uttered the word "autism." I do recall that I couldn't repeat it for months afterward. I didn't know what it meant; I just knew it wasn't good. I learned it was something bigger than I could have ever imagined; that it wrought changes in my life I would never have anticipated, pushing me to limits I didn't know that I had; and that it can be an extremely isolating disorder.

.

Recently, my sense of isolation yielded to one of solidarity. When I wrote about the drowning death of a young boy with autism, I heard from many strangers—mothers, grandmothers, and aunts—whose worlds were also rocked by an autism diagnosis. I found I was part of a sisterhood, and that filled me with a sense of solidarity—and sadness. I learned we shared my feelings of isolation, and that they, too, had lived in fear and desperation for years. There was a painful theme: No one understands what it means to have a family member with autism. And they were grateful I'd shared our story.

So here I am again. I am no expert, no professional. I can only tell my story.

For years, from the moment he woke up to the moment he fell asleep (for sleep was an ongoing challenge), Jack's needs, actions, and whereabouts were always on my mind—almost like having a busy toddler who never grew up. When he was very young, our family life was like a roller coaster propelled by his moods, activity level, and chronic sleeplessness. Each day was unpredictable.

I spent years hoping I would find a magic bullet that would cure him and restore our lives to "normalcy." I took him to more than fifty healthcare professionals to address his developmental delays and chronic, complicated, and confusing medical issues. We saw neurologists, psychologists, psychiatrists, pediatricians, gastroenterologists, urologists, cardiologists, orthopedists, and speech, occupational, and vision therapists.

I filled out dozens of medical forms, each time reliving the heartache as I recounted his development and regression, reported his symptoms and related the treatments we'd tried, embraced, and/or discarded. Many days, I bit my tongue to keep from screaming, "Can't someone develop a universal medical form?"

Gradually, Jack's medical issues dissipated, and his behavior improved. We no longer had to worry about whether he could eat pizza without vomiting on the sidewalk outside the restaurant, or whether we would fall asleep before he did. He began to speak more

•

and move less. He became more aware of social cues and more willing to engage in social interactions. We will never know if there was a magic bullet, because in my quest for normalcy, I tried so many therapies, medications, diets, and supplements simultaneously, it was impossible to ascertain what worked and what failed. The process certainly wasn't optimal; but the results offered shards of hope.

Worrisome Isolation

AS JACK AGED and matured, I did some growing of my own. I began to focus more on his positive attributes—his sweet disposition and dry sense of humor—and less on his challenges. I was moving beyond my pain over things that likely matter more to me than to him, like having friends. Where I once felt desperation, I now felt acceptance, accompanied by a lighter heart.

After years of sending a notebook back and forth to teachers who recounted Jack's challenges and successes (more the former than the latter), it was refreshing to have a middle school teacher who not only had a sense of humor, but also enjoyed Jack's.

Anne Barnes kept a running list of humorous comments by Jack that she shared with us periodically. My favorite was when the fifth-grade class began a drug and alcohol prevention program called DARE. Jack had an announcement for his classmates and the staff.

"I don't think Mom and Dad are going to like DARE very much. I have to take them off the beer."

When Jack transitioned from middle school to a considerably larger high school, he continued to spend most of the day in a special education room. Attempts to involve him in extracurricular activities at a school that advertised a plethora of options fell short. He attended one meeting of the drama club. It didn't go well. I never heard what transpired: just that he wasn't welcome to return. My request for an upperclassman to mentor him in the drama club fell on deaf ears, along with my suggestion that he hand out programs at the performance. I was angry, defeated, and deflated. I'd gotten my hopes up that high school would open doors that might lead to at least one friendship.

Jack's isolation became worrisome. At the end of the school day, he would return home and isolate himself in his bedroom, with video games as his companions. I found it difficult to discern whether his withdrawal was due to adolescence or autism, or some combination thereof. He later revealed he was being bullied at school.

Though he spent most of the school day in the special education room with students who had a variety of challenges, he also attended one or two mainstream classes. At the end of his freshman year, I asked him which setting felt right.

"The kids in the resource room are too immature. The kids in the other class don't have my mental disability," he replied.

It was distressing to hear our child say he does not feel like he belongs anywhere. Social isolation is dangerous for teens, and I feared where it might lead our son, who professed to have PSE (his own acronym for poor self-esteem). Hours spent alone in his bedroom surfing the Internet or playing video games suited him, but distressed Ted and me.

A series of conversations prompted my search for a different school. Locally, I found nothing. Days before summer's end, I learned about a boarding school in rural New Hampshire.

When we learned of it, Hampshire Country School catered to young males with a variety of challenges and talents. Most entered when they were in middle school. Instead of video games, students at Hampshire Country School played board games and chess. They canoed on the lake and hiked through the woods. They developed social skills and manners, because that's what happens when you share meals and chores, and learn and recreate together.

While some parents of struggling teens might give such an opportunity fleeting consideration, Ted and I saw this haven of other bright, but lonely, boys, who didn't fit into the mainstream, as the answer to our prayers. The three of us made a quick visit to the campus and met with the headmaster. As a private school, HCS has no government-mandated education plans or special education teachers. Though at sixteen, Jack was much older than the typical new student, the headmaster saw potential and opportunity, and invited him to attend.

After our visit I asked Jack what he thought about going to HCS. He gave me the "thumbs up" sign and continued eating his breakfast. That was all I needed. I shifted into high gear, racing from the clothing store to the doctor's office, purchasing airline tickets and packing. Ted and I enrolled Jack at HCS with encouragement from other parents, a new loan, and prayers on our lips.

You've Got a Friend

JUST NINE DAYS after learning about Hampshire Country School, I drove through the breathtaking beauty of New Hampshire with my silent companion at my side, his bags packed. The intellectual analysis that drove the decision to send him there receded into the back of my mind, and my motherly instincts took over.

The wrenching realization that I was taking our son, for whom I had devoted the previous sixteen years of my life, across the country to live with complete strangers who knew nothing about his habits, his idiosyncrasies, or his needs, finally struck me. The school's approach—you step back, we step in—suddenly seemed fraught with risk. Had I, the air traffic controller of this boy's life, actually advocated for this?

Almost on cue, the radio began playing a favorite tune from my youth, "You've Got a Friend." As James Taylor sang the familiar lyrics, "*Winter, spring, summer or fall, all you need to do is call and I'll be there . . . ,*" tears streamed down my face. I realized how desperately I wanted this to be true for Jack. Though I already had the intellectual resolve I needed for the decision, the song's lyrics gave me the emotional affirmation that I was on the right road.

Scores of parenting decisions had prepared me for this pivotal moment. In a huge leap of faith, I accepted that I had to extract our son from his solitude and deliver him to strangers in the hope he would find a friend. So ignoring Jack's last-minute plea not to leave him at the "old fashioned school," I took a deep breath and did just that.

In the days that passed after we said our painful good-byes, I feared my heart would burst from the pain. Knowing Jack was struggling, too, I prayed he would find a buddy in the beautiful foothills of the Monadnock Mountains and stop wondering why his parents had sent him there.

When a child is college bound, his parents have ample opportunity to ready themselves for his departure. Because we didn't expect Jack to attend college, much less boarding school, we were unprepared for the emotional separation.

Over time I became more comfortable with the quiet that overtook our household in Jack's absence. I developed a new appreciation for time. Time helps us to prepare, heal, and gain perspective. I saw how autism had dominated our family life; how Jack's needs had remained constant as his siblings' needs had evolved and matured in tandem with the development of skills, independence, and a desire to assert both. I saw how my focus on Jack's needs may have both facilitated and limited his development, and how it made me less available to others who also needed me.

Hampshire Country School limits students' contact with the outside world, especially at the beginning of the school year. Students need time and space to adapt to a new home and school, as well as to different routines and expectations.

Jack had no access to a computer or cellphone, and minimal contact with home. Instead, he had pencil, paper, envelopes, and stamps, and a school requirement that he use them weekly. I knew I would have a letter, however cryptic, in my mailbox at week's end. He, in turn, could expect regular letters from both parents, occasional packages from me, and periodic notes from other family members and friends.

It wasn't long before we discovered how difficult it was to maintain a fluid dialogue by snail mail. In his first letter home, Jack (an avid reader) asked me to send him a new book. I wrote back to clarify which book he wanted and awaited a reply that never arrived. I don't know if he missed my question or ignored it, but weeks later I learned what he was waiting for.

> *Dear Mom and Dad,*
>
> *I miss you very much. I have got your stuff so please for the love of God, send me Scorpia. How hard is it for you to understand? Go to a bookstore, mall, Target or Walmart. Hell, go to Kmart or Sears. I just want the book. Sorry for snapping. I am just getting pissed off. I want to know what happened between Eagle Strike and Ark Angel. I just want some new reading material. Why did you send me the crossword book? I didn't even ask for that. I just threw it in my trash . . . I seriously feel like you are ignoring my letters or just not reading them. That is all I have to say. Hope to see you. Love, Jack*

Not reading his letters? I devoured every one, always saddened that he ended them by saying he hoped to see us and by asking if our dog Sara was doing okay. Clearly, as I waited for his reply to my question, he waited for the book. The relative time warp of snail mail made it impossible to clarify something so simple.

How did we function before electronic communication?

The Magic Forest

FIFTY-NINE DAYS after I left him at school, Ted and I saw Jack on our first parents' weekend. He was two inches taller and ten pounds lighter and had clearly matured.

"I was angry at you for leaving me here," he said as he released me from his bear hug. "Then I realized why you did it."

"Why?" I asked, both eager for and fearful of his answer.

"Because you love me."

I was stunned that an adolescent male, particularly one with a social communication disorder, would be so clear in his thoughts and his words. More than that, I was thrilled he seemed to have found his place and understood the rationale behind his abrupt and unanticipated move.

Jack was eager to introduce us to his new friends—Max, a six-year-old boy with autism, and his mom, a dorm parent who clearly had become my son's surrogate mom. Mrs. D led the daily hikes our former couch potato now enjoyed. She was quick to share how much she appreciated our son's kindness to hers. Equally grateful for her kindness to Jack, I felt an instant bond with her.

Jack confirmed that he and Max were tight. "He is the little brother I always wanted, but never had."

All weekend I watched Jack with Max. I saw his kindness, humor, concern, and affection, encouraged that he had the skills and inclination, but aware he was using them on someone ten years his junior, rather than a boy his own age. I tried to subtly encourage him to let his peers see those qualities as well.

When we attended parent/teacher conferences, we were thrilled to learn that by week six Jack was learning long division, after spending years working mostly on time and money worksheets in the special education rooms at his prior schools. Though he was prone to outbursts and tended to swear a lot in Spanish class, he was emerging from his shell, beginning to relax and to participate.

In time, he adjusted to the dramatic changes. He participated in family-style meals with students, faculty, and staff. He was forced into social interactions. He began to eat foods he would have rejected at home. As he walked miles every day, he developed new muscles and stamina. He had issues with various classmates, as he had at home, but learned to coexist with a small group of people with whom he spent all day every day.

While living at home, Jack spent hours with his fingers on a keyboard or a remote control. With electronic entertainment taboo at HCS, he discovered his creative side, as a writer and an artist. On parents' weekend, he revealed it. During lunch we noticed paintings bearing his signature hanging from the dining room walls. Featuring vivid colors and robust brush strokes, his work was clearly inspired by *anime*, the Japanese art form reflected in his large Pokémon card collection. "He has real talent," his art teacher said.

The highlight of the weekend was when the boy who often spoke softly and haltingly participated in the student talent show. He stood before an audience of mostly strangers and, in a pristine voice, read a poem he had written for the occasion.

The Magic Forest

The magic forest, with trees so blue and sky so green,
Where yales and unicorns frolic freely
Where phoenixes and dragons and Pegasi and griffins and
Hippogriffs and rocs fly,
Where jabberwocks and gerrymanders and basilisks slither,
Yes, the magic forest, where satyrs and fauns and centaurs
    meet in peace;
Where hippocampi, mermaids, and krakens swim
Where Ents roam and leprechauns dance;
The magic forest, where Minotaurs graze,
Where big feet and abominable snowmen roam;
The magic forest, with fields of purple and streams of orange,
With corn of silver and potatoes of gold;
The magic forest, where you can fly.
Just believe what you want to believe.
The magic forest. It exists only in my imagination.

Jack Sullivan

The Mortification Zone

WE ENROLLED JACK in Hampshire Country School because we felt
it was the best place for him to acquire academic and social skills
in the waning years of high school. We hadn't considered how his
absence would alter life at home.

Ted, Julia, and I gradually adapted to a life unknown to all of us,
devoid of the person who was clearly the hub in the family wheel.
When Jack returned to Minnesota at the end of the school year, we
adapted again, as families do. We had a new frame of reference and
appreciation for how Jack's behavior affected us.

When the *Pioneer Press* ran an article about how kids will em-
barrass their parents, I weighed in on a familiar topic.

• • •

I have to believe that other families dealing with conditions such as
autism, Tourette syndrome, ADHD, or Alzheimer's are acquainted
with the mortification zone, where I've often dwelled. Since I have
a relatively low threshold for embarrassment, I've been mortified
by my guy's behavior on countless occasions. Is he to blame? He
arrived without a filter to stop him from blurting out comments, or
doing things others might consider, but reject.

I feel guilty because I know the nuances of what is cool and what
is taboo are confusing, and the line between entertainment and embarrassment is fuzzy for him. Yet, I also know he relishes making
outrageous comments. Always the entertainer, he can't comprehend

why we laugh when comedian Jim Carrey talks with his butt cheeks in *Ace Ventura: Pet Detective*, but gasp when he mimics the actor in the crowded Chicago Shedd Aquarium—with his shorts around his ankles.

If I don't always know how to interpret or respond to his behavior, how can I expect strangers to be any wiser? I've often longed for a symbol like a wheelchair or white cane to broadcast his challenges. Absent that, I constantly run interference to protect him and the rest of the family from others' misunderstanding or judgment. Lately, I'm wondering whether I'm observing the unintended consequences of excessive coaching, reflected in his high anxiety, low self-esteem, and defiant behaviors. Is it time to accept that he is who he is?

Rather than being mortified, I am starting to think of Jack as our personal color commentator on life, like a retired hoopster who sits in a booth during basketball games, adding flavor to the broadcast. He's a complex guy who causes my heart to twist and turn. He nearly put me under the table when he told our new friends that everyone who read *The Da Vinci Code* knows "Jesus was banging Mary Magdalene."

But he made my heart soar when he performed a stand-up comedy routine at his boarding school. He's my self-proclaimed "man child," who loudly told his brother to check out a woman's cleavage, then noted, "Mom, you have bags under your eyes . . . but you're still beautiful."

I see that I have a choice about how I relate to him. I can embrace the lighter moments and ignore the embarrassing ones. As to others, I can establish a context for his behavior so they might be less offended or hurt if he ignores their attempts at conversation, or points out the obvious when no one else dares. For him, I can keep trying, gently, to impress upon him that good manners are important and that others' feelings matter, too.

Don't Try to Fix Me

WITH JACK IN NEW HAMPSHIRE for a second year, my goals and perspective continued to shift. The psychologist's prediction that he could become "normal" by high school was rapidly losing traction, supplanted by a reluctant acceptance of reality. As I began to look at Jack's autism less as a dream thief, and more as a permanent condition, my writing assumed a new tone.

In April of 2009, on World Autism Awareness Day, I saluted my fellow travelers, as well as their children, as I wrote about my changing attitude.

• • •

For years, I desperately devoted most of my time, energy, and resources to snatching our son from the jaws of autism. One day, he overheard me talking with a scientist friend about the potential causes of and cures for autism. Indignantly, he said to me, "Autism is not a disease . . . it's a condition."

It struck me that he knew himself better than I did, and he was drawing a line, saying, "This is who I am. Don't try to fix me." His statement haunted me, forcing me to evaluate my objective.

I've come to appreciate that Jack is first a person, and secondly a person with autism. For him, that means he has a condition that affects his ability and desire to sustain interpersonal relationships, to execute tasks that are second nature to most, and to control his attention, energy, and emotions. That insight was my salvation. It helped me to stop fighting the invisible demon. Disengaged from the fight for the fix, I have focused instead on doing for him what I have done for his siblings: helping him to develop skills and potential through the best education and support we can manage.

Taking his lead, I have evolved from a parent determined to fix her child so he was like his older brother—smart, athletic, engaged in the world and with the people around him—to one who has mostly accepted him for who he is. We may never have deep conversations about books or politics, as I do with his brother, but I can nevertheless have a different and meaningful bond with him.

Our relationship has inspired many of the most valuable lessons I have learned in life. To cope with a condition I scarcely understand, I have expanded my black-and-white worldview to make room for gray, uncertainty, and unpredictability. Together, Jack and I have learned to be patient, when it is contrary to our nature to be so. I have developed compassion I lacked before I was exposed to a world in which challenges are the rule, not the exception. I have set new standards for judging my son's progress and success; by doing so, I can joyfully celebrate achievements that would be unremarkable for his siblings, but are outstanding for him.

If life had proceeded as we expected when Jack was born, we would have shared in the activities that consume families as high school comes to an end—sorting through post-secondary options, preparing for prom, and undergoing the battles that are part of the painful separation that precedes a departure from the family nest. But Jack never attended a high school dance. There were no plans for him after he finished school. He was happiest living at home.

Many times over the years my heart throbbed when friends discussed their kids' athletic and academic successes and busy social lives. Fortunately, acceptance has delivered the peace that serves as a formidable antidote to my nemesis—bitterness—and helps me to be gracious about others' accomplishments.

I'm Basically Screwed

THOUGH JACK made good progress, he still lagged behind other teens. He couldn't manage money, had no interest in driving, and was vulnerable on many fronts. We decided it was in his best interest to establish legal guardianship for him: a painful process that prompted a column in which I exposed my vulnerability.

• • •

Helping our children to feel both grounded and independent is a fundamental tenet of parenting. So we give them roots and wings by imparting skills and values. We harp on them to buckle their seat belts, eat their veggies, and treat others with respect. After we have counseled them on how to do their homework and manage money and relationships, we guide them toward a college or career path, with the expectation that when they reach adulthood, we will step away as they launch their independent lives . . . except when they have special needs.

With the passage of time, the expectation of Jack's emancipation passed through my fingers like the sand in an hourglass. With his eighteenth birthday on the horizon, we prepared by taking him to court.

On an August morning in 2008, we walked into a packed courtroom and relinquished the dream that the therapies, diets, medications, and strategies we had employed since his diagnosis would rewire his brain and render him a typically functioning man who

•

would attend college, find a job, marry the love of his life, and become a father.

As we sat in the courtroom, surrounded by acquaintances that were also there, coincidentally, to handle their own legal matters, I felt exposed. I had not expected there to be so many familiar faces witnessing my moment of reckoning, much less the tears I could not control. There it was for all to witness—my full court press to guarantee my son's independence had not been adequate after all. The judge would order the outcome and it would become part of the permanent court record.

When a child receives an autism diagnosis, his loved ones experience a loss that may not be well defined but is deeply felt. As the years passed, it became evident we would not only forfeit some of our dreams, we would also forfeit a future free from responsibility. Committed to ensuring roots were intact, even if wings could not soar, we accepted responsibility for managing Jack's well-being for the foreseeable future: his medical care, his money, his living arrangements, and any contractual obligations.

My heart was heavy when we left the courtroom. I imagined a retractable leash stretched between my son and me, tethering us forever. Yet Jack was not sad. He was relieved, because the guardianship offered a sense of security, much like the seat belt he never fails to engage.

The court appearance exemplified the disparate emotions I've felt over the years. At the beginning of the proceedings, I couldn't hold back my tears. But at its conclusion I, along with others in the courtroom, enjoyed a welcome laugh when Jack added levity to a heavy moment.

When the judge asked Jack if he agreed with the guardianship arrangement, he replied very earnestly, "Yes, Judge, because without my parents making my major life decisions, I'm basically screwed."

●

Temple Grandin: Different, Not Less

THOUGH I VALUE the insights of other parents, I especially appreciate those of adults with autism, such as John Elder Robison (author of *Look Me in the Eye* and *Cubby's Dad*) and Temple Grandin. In 2010 *Time* magazine included Temple in its list of 100 people who most affect our world, citing her influence as both a renowned animal scientist, and an inspirational advocate for people with autism.

With an award-winning HBO film depicting her life, frequent media interviews, books, and speeches, Temple has become, for many, the most well-recognized face and voice of autism. Yet the Colorado State University professor defines herself as first an animal scientist, designer, and professor, then a person with autism. She is renowned for developing a deep touch pressure device, called a squeeze machine, to help her cope with her sensory overload and nervousness.

I interviewed Temple twice when she was in the Twin Cities for speaking engagements. When we met in February of 2011, I was hoping to glean some nuggets from someone who had become skilled at expressing herself. Sporting her trademark Western-style blouse and bolero, she was engaging, articulate, and direct.

Born in 1947, Temple was initially thought to have brain damage. Her mother reported she engaged in destructive behavior, was sensitive to touch, and fixated on spinning objects. Temple didn't speak until she was four years old. Her father wanted to put her in an institution, but her mother refused and taught her at home instead.

Temple credits her mother with pushing her to develop speech, manners, and a work ethic.

In her youth she held many jobs, ranging from sewing to cleaning horse barns. Her jobs taught her about both the fun and grunt work that employment entails. She learned how to perform tasks that superiors assigned, even if she wasn't interested in doing them.

Temple describes herself as a visual thinker who uses specific examples to create concepts. She likens her mind to a search engine. She is more about what she does than what she feels (though she recognizes that is a difficult concept for "social people" to grasp). She is well aware of both the strengths and limitations inherent in her autism. She wouldn't change the way it enables her to view the world, and doesn't let it define or consume her.

Many older people, presumably on the autism spectrum, are successfully employed, often in Silicon Valley. They've managed to get by in the workplace because they were from a generation that emphasized manners and social skills. She adds, "They've had enough social skills bashed into them, so they know better."

Temple learned early in her career to sell her work, not her personality. She also learned to focus on the work she was hired to do, and to keep her distance from everything else. Her boss taught her a humiliating lesson about hygiene when he slammed a can of deodorant on a desk and insisted she use it. Initially angry, she became grateful, recognizing that while it is okay to be eccentric, it is not okay to be a "rude, dirty slob."

Consulting and speaking engagements consume much of Temple's time. Her experience and success, coupled with her candor, appeal to conference, school, and commencement audiences, who soak up her explanations about medications, sensory challenges, and difficulties with sequencing and organizing.

She has become a valuable resource for professionals and parents who wonder why children flap their hands and avoid eye contact, and whether parents should respect a child's penchant for isolation. Yet she worries that too many people approach her for advice about their autism. She'd rather hear about their interests or activities. She encourages them to parlay fixations or interests into hobbies or jobs, as she did with her fascination with cattle chutes.

To her mind, many parents are overprotective and do a poor job of preparing their kids for adulthood. Manners, part of the 1950's social curriculum, have gone astray. Consequently, kids who approach her at book signings don't know how to shake hands or to request an autograph. Their parents often speak for them. And that annoys her.

Knowing she had attended Hampshire Country School when it was co-ed, I mentioned that Jack had spent three years there. Temple immediately peppered me with questions about Jack, returning to him throughout our interview. "What does he like to do? Is he a good reader? Does he like to write? What are his hobbies?"

I had grappled with how to prepare Jack for adulthood. Temple had many suggestions, mostly about things we should have done years earlier. Start a blog for him. Get a job for him. Help him to develop friendships with peers with shared interests by encouraging him to join clubs or take up extracurricular activities, such as robotics or art.

The rapid-fire questions and comments about Jack were well intentioned, illuminating, and instructive. Yet, as I digested them, I became increasingly distressed. There was no avoiding it: despite all my efforts, I hadn't exhausted the possibilities for my son. But I was exhausted.

As much as I appreciated the suggestions, I was left with a troubling thought. Does a parent of a special needs child ever feel she's done enough?

Through Jimmy's Eyes

WHILE MY FAMILY was learning about autism and dealing with Jack's medical issues, Peg and Brian Reagan were on a parallel path with their son Jimmy. Several years ago, they made a discovery that not only transformed Jimmy, but also changed the dynamics and focus in their household.

Jimmy Reagan's story unfolds through pictures. It begins with baby photos his parents treasure: Jimmy as an infant, snacking in his high chair, impish grin stretching between rosy cheeks; Jimmy frolicking with his dad in a pile of leaves, bright eyes focused on the camera. Then the images reflect a dramatic change. Jimmy the toddler is no longer laughing and snuggling with older siblings. His smile has faded. Black circles underscore his vacant eyes.

Somewhere around his second birthday, Jimmy regressed from a typically developing child, to one who is living with autism. Although his parents cannot explain their child's regression, it is highlighted by atypical conversational skills and social interaction.

The years following Jimmy's 1996 diagnosis were frightening and frustrating. Along with social and communication deficits, Jimmy experienced incapacitating health problems that eluded diagnosis and treatment. He lost so much weight his older brother worried that Jimmy was dying before their eyes. Jack Reagan implored his parents to do something.

Midway through eighth grade, his parents withdrew Jimmy from school. Over time, doctors began to understand and address his various ailments. Jimmy's chronic pain subsided. Though his appearance improved, his language didn't return.

By pure accident, Jimmy's teacher and her artist friend discovered the young man with limited verbal skills had a penchant for art. Jimmy began working with paintbrushes and colored pencils. He visited museums, read art books, and took art classes.

A fan of Vincent Van Gogh's work, Jimmy has generated an impressive collection of landscapes and portraits. He produces multiple pieces reflecting different perspectives of the same scene or object, no two alike.

The portfolio of this emerging artist is marked by short lines called tick marks and vivid colors juxtaposed to make them pop. No longer chasing medical diagnoses, Peg helps Jimmy to develop and market his artwork. They display it around the Twin Cities and sell it on his website. His renditions appear on canvas, prints, note cards, scarves, ties, T-shirts, and handbags.

For Peg, identifying and nurturing talent is the ticket to a meaningful and productive life for all her kids; but discovering Jimmy's aptitude for art has been especially promising, considering the unique, lifelong challenges his autism presents. She notes that while some people are miserable in their jobs, Jim does something that he loves, that people appreciate, and that earns him respect. Though he is a man of few words, his gift enables family, friends, and fans to see the world through Jimmy's eyes.

Witnessing Jimmy's transformation motivated me to continue opening doors for Jack. He reluctantly agreed to take an improv class. He enthusiastically decided to spend an hour per week with a local artist who is helping him to transform his rudimentary drawings. He continues to spend hours composing romantic stories—

without punctuation. "The words flow through my brain so fast I can't figure out the punctuation," he reports. So I've encouraged him to pursue poetry.

It makes sense that Jimmy and Jack would be late bloomers, given their developmental delays. We've planted the seeds, watered and fertilized the soil. Now it is time to step back and watch as the petals unfold, stretch, and reveal their beauty.

part
five

Reflections

The Healing Power of Words

THOUGH I BEGAN writing about autism, I came to understand that the need—the desire—for awareness, insight, and acceptance was not exclusive to families living with the mysterious condition. We are all grappling to get to life's finish line without a playbook. The more people I meet, the clearer it becomes: everyone has stuff. Not everyone shares it in blogs, books, or newspapers, but it is there. Hints of it seep out after a glass of wine, or through an unguarded expression.

The anthology, *Special Gifts: Women Writers on the Heartache, the Happiness and the Hope of Raising a Special Needs Child*, demonstrated that sharing the heartache is important; it raises awareness and, hopefully, creates compassion. Our capacity for processing negative news is continuously taxed by news reports about terrorists beheading civilians, priests abusing children, and politicians spending more time pointing fingers at opponents than governing. Human beings crave happiness and hope.

I began to write about other insights and experiences in my own life, as well as to seek out interesting people and organizations dedicated to helping others. They inspire hope through action and opportunity.

Often chatting over coffee, I've met with employees and volunteers who helped storm victims, students, and uneducated African women, occasionally in the spotlight, but mostly under the radar.

They've stretched themselves by donating bone marrow; mentoring children; providing hearing aids to those who could not afford them in countries many would hesitate to visit; and donating books, school supplies, and toiletries to those in need.

I also began to illuminate struggles about which people tend to be private: military life, mental illness, addiction, Alzheimer's, eating disorders, and myriad health conditions. Though most columns involve people or organizations in Minnesota, they could just as easily have emanated from California or Maine. The setting is incidental to the message.

Themes emerged. The people who are living interesting lives, navigating challenges, and overcoming adversity, make choices, consciously or not. They bring a positive attitude to simple and complex situations. They find strength and comfort in solidarity. They are humble; they acknowledge mistakes; and they focus outward more than inward.

They place a high value on being students of life, learning from what works and what does not. They count humor among the essentials in their toolkits. Whether they realize it or not, they are crafting their legacies.

I count these strangers among the angels who carried me after I became a widow. Their strength, tenacity, and selflessness helped me to throw my shoulders back and soldier on: to be a survivor with a message, rather than a victim with an empty life.

I continue to search for new stories, and when time and opportunity permit, to support the causes that most interest me. Ever mindful of the people who helped my family during our crises, I am committed to being generous with others, as they have been with my loved ones and me.

There is also a selfish motivation. Writing about how others deal with the tough stuff distracts me from my own woes, and offers perspective too valuable not to share.

What follows is a collection of some of my favorite stories, most of which appeared in the St. Paul *Pioneer Press*. Writing has been instrumental in preparing me for, and helping me to grow from, adversity. Each person and experience I've written about has contributed to the patchwork quilt of my life—a thread here, a square there. Strung together, the stories reveal a recipe for navigating life.

Life Isn't Fair

WHEN WE WERE GROWING UP, we didn't celebrate Mother's Day with my mother, for she considered it a "made-up holiday." Its purpose, she insisted, was to generate sales for greeting card and candy companies during their slow business cycles. While that may have been the impetus behind the holiday, I think there is value in acknowledging our mothers.

In May of 2008, I wrote a column about Mother's Day that, in retrospect, helped to prepare me for more tough stuff.

•　•　•

I won't be taking my mom to brunch or sending her flowers on this Mother's Day. I lost her years before I became a mother myself. In years past, I've been melancholic on this day, as I've brooded over how much I've needed her in my life, feeling cheated by the little time I had with her before she succumbed to cancer. But this year, having just marked five years without cancer in my own body, I've been grateful for the most valuable lesson she taught me.

My childhood was rockier than many, my parents' divorces and deaths landing at my feet with a resounding thud that left a lasting impact on my psyche. To her last breath, my mother was unwavering in her oft-stated conviction that life isn't fair. With her words in my pocket, I was able to move beyond the tough stuff of my youth without becoming paralyzed, or feeling victimized.

•

As an adult, I've thought she must have been clairvoyant, as I've had to rely on her words at regular intervals. They've helped me to focus my energy on activism, not anger, since my firstborn was diagnosed with autism. They steadied me when my marathoner husband had his first heart attack. They gave me the resolve to meet my own cancer diagnosis with a defiant conviction, "I'm not going to die from this." Above all, her words deflected the bitterness that fought to camp on my doorstep when our ten-year-old daughter became seriously ill.

Friends have asked whether I feel I've been given more than my fair share to deal with. How could I say yes, with my mother's words so firmly ensconced in my soul?

That's not to say it's been easy. I've been exhausted, depressed, and overwhelmed, incredulous that my life is what it is. At times I've fought off intense feelings of envy as I've looked around and noted how others' lives seem to go more smoothly. Yet, over time, I've made my peace, realizing that while I can't control autism or illness, I can control my attitude and my behavior. I see that everyone has their struggles, some more transparent than others.

I'm mindful of how challenges have enriched my life in unexpected ways. Like my mother, I always planned to have a career. But with an autism diagnosis in hand and another baby on the way, I abruptly changed hats and became the stay-at-home mom I was raised not to be. I've spent far more time with my children than I ever spent with my mother, unconsciously patching a hole in my soul.

My kids (the two I gave birth to and the two who came as a package deal with their father) have had many ups and downs as a blended family with a special needs child. They have quietly and courageously faced challenges, big and small. Living with them has made me a more compassionate, patient, and hopeful person.

In their own way, each of them has demonstrated that advanced degrees and financial wealth are not the exclusive barometers of success. I am proud of their accomplishments, whether it be graduating college and landing a good job with benefits; facing daunting medical, social, or scholastic hurdles; or holding out for the ideal life partner. I pray their lives are filled with great joy. But when they experience heartache, as we all do, I hope they will reach into their pockets and retrieve the same words that have bolstered me in difficult times. And I hope they will always remember to send me a Mother's Day card.

The Worst-Case Scenario

AS MY LOVED ONES and I successfully repelled medical challenges, I felt like a warrior dodging bullets on a battlefield. How long would our luck hold out? After each crisis, each angioplasty, I waited for another shoe to drop. I indulged fleeting thoughts about Ted's mortality. Yet, we rarely discussed the cloud that hovered above us.

In mid-July 2007, I was driving on the road behind our home when I struck a vehicle whose driver pulled out in front of me. My Trailblazer careened off the road, coming to an abrupt stop when it struck a tree. Both my vehicle and the tree buckled from the impact.

In the days that followed, my thoughts lingered on how the other driver and I would likely have landed in the morgue, instead of the emergency room, without air bags and seat belts to brace the impact. Angry and depressed, I dwelled on one detail—if I'd taken my usual route to pick up Ted at the airport, the accident wouldn't have happened.

My family was also rattled by my accident. I heard the fear in my typically reserved daughter's voice when she said she loved me. I sensed the same worry in her older siblings, who viewed the photo of my smashed vehicle on their cellphones and called from afar. Jack welcomed me home from the hospital by loaning me his cobra statue to protect me from demons. Ted arrived by cab at the hospital, shell-shocked but relieved that, while the vehicle was totaled, I was intact.

Not long after my accident, Minneapolis experienced a much

more serious trauma when an interstate bridge collapsed during rush hour, not far from the stadium where baseball fans had gathered to watch the Minnesota Twins. Thoughts about my personal scare evaporated when I saw images of the I-35W bridge jutting out of the mighty Mississippi River. Watching footage of the trucks, cars, and a school bus suspended on the bridge and submerged in the river, my personal concerns seemed trivial. With a truly remarkable disaster at hand, my focus, like millions around the world, shifted to the families whose lives were shattered when the unthinkable occurred that evening.

The concrete bridge, a presumably intractable structure, faltered, then failed. Recalling how frightened I was when I realized my car crash was inevitable, I couldn't imagine how terrified both survivors and victims must have felt when the bridge shuddered, then split, with them on it. My accident wasn't particularly unusual— a novice driver, looking the wrong way, pulled out in front of me. But no one expects a major bridge that spans the Mississippi River to split in two.

As I read stories about the adult victims, my mind was immediately drawn to their children, who'd lost a parent in the freak accident. I knew about the hollow moments they would endure without parents who should be there. I knew how hard it might be for their hearts to heal.

Among the survivors there would be many walking wounded— those who would be unable to put the sounds and images of the collapse out of their minds for a long time; those who would be unable to drive across bridges because they couldn't escape the horror of what they experienced on August 2, 2007; those who couldn't comprehend how they made it safely to the other side. I hoped they would find a cobra to fight off their demons, like the one my son had offered to me.

I wondered if other families were better prepared than ours for life after an unforeseen tragedy. I wrestled with this issue with no resolution. If something happened to Ted and me, Jack would have a rough road to traverse. In contrast to his three siblings, his goal was not to get through high school, into college, and onto an independent life. He'd need help with transitioning from high school to an unknown destination—school, vocational training, or work—as well as with suitable housing, recurring medical issues, complicated social challenges, and ongoing financial support.

Every family has unique circumstances. They may be blended, military, or have elderly or infirm relatives, all factors to consider when planning for the future. Contemplating and discussing alternatives and financing can be stressful and strain relationships. Yet, my accident and the bridge collapse offer callous reminders that there is no upside to avoiding difficult discussions or decisions. Much as we'd prefer not to think about it, we all need a plan for the worst-case scenario.

Tony Snow's Unwavering Spirit

I STUDIED JOURNALISM when news was reported in the news section, and opinions were shared on the opinion page. Sadly, that line has blurred in the years since I obtained my degree. But the rules were well ingrained in me. When I consume the news, I favor the anchors and reporters who had the same training; particularly those who inform, rather than inflame, their viewers.

Tony Snow was one of my favorites. When he died of cancer in July 2008 at age fifty-three, I felt as if I'd lost a kindred spirit to a familiar disease. It's rather odd to feel a sense of loss for someone I never met. In his roles as radio and TV commentator, writer, and George W. Bush spokesman, Tony was refreshingly humble and engaging. He had a sparkle in his eye and a lilt in his voice. He was smart, funny, provocative, and respectful to all, regardless of political persuasion. As a musician, film lover, and family man, he lived life with vigor. He was a rare celebrity who, according to those who knew him, never changed after becoming famous.

On summer weekend mornings, Ted and I went biking with a group of our neighbors. The guys were known as the Copperfield Clydesdales and I (the sole female rider) as the pony. After I heard the news about Tony, I rolled out of bed, put on my spandex shorts and helmet and joined the Clydesdales on a trek into a twenty mph wind.

As we rode up and down the hills, I thought about how much biking is like fighting cancer—and navigating life. Some days the wind is relentless; other days it's calm. There are times to coast and times to crank the gears and use every bit of energy to climb a seemingly insurmountable hill. The exhilaration of making it to the top provides the fuel for the next hill.

I thought about the ups and downs that Tony had been through since his diagnosis in 2005, and how, despite his conviction that optimism is a potent weapon against the disease, he didn't make it to the top of that last hill. I thought about his school-age kids, who'd lost their dad at such an important time in their lives, and about his wife, who lost a special guy far too early. I thought about how those of us who had admired him from afar had lost an exceptional role model in a public arena more typically full of big egos and questionable values.

On Sunday morning, I skipped the bike ride, opting to watch as Tony's colleagues paid tribute to him on his former show, *Fox News Sunday*. I looked at picture after picture of him with a smile on his face, even after his hair disappeared and his frame dwindled. Though the treatment and the disease took their toll on his body, his spirit seemed invincible. I wondered whether a person is born with that unwavering cheerful outlook, or if it's possible to acquire it. I wish I had more of it.

Ted died eighteen months after Tony. Though he hadn't battled cancer, he'd been climbing his own hill with his heart problems. Each time he went to the cardiologist or checked into the hospital, we waited breathlessly for the outcome. I imagine he lived his final years in the shadow of the inevitable. The parallels in the lives of two remarkable men serve as a reminder that while we may follow different paths through life, we all arrive at the same destination.

Roadmap to a Life Well-Lived

ON NEW YEAR'S EVE 2009, a small group of friends gathered at Ann and John McDonald's home to send off a year that had ended dismally, and to welcome one we hoped would bring healing. As we relaxed at the dinner table, the conversation turned to my writing. In his notoriously impish style, John teased, "Your columns are always about you, Caryn, always about you."

In early 2010, I couldn't summon the energy, or the words, to produce any columns. But inspiration struck in March, and I composed what became my favorite column. I regret that neither John nor Ted were able to read "Roadmap to a Life Well Lived," for it was my tribute to two friends, colleagues, neighbors, and competitors.

• • •

It's curious how we live life in denial, disregard, or even defiance of the one thing that is certain to occur to all. Death. It's been twelve weeks since I got a phone call I hadn't anticipated. My husband Ted, bearer of seven stents and survivor of a previous heart attack, died on his way home from the health club while I was out of state. He had promised his friend John that, "barring a catastrophe," he would join him for dinner.

John's wife, Ann, became my steadfast companion. Ann helped me to navigate tasks that in ordinary times would be simple to accomplish, but in a grief-stricken, sleep-deprived state feel overwhelming: preparing meals, dealing with Social Security, submitting

•

life insurance claims, changing vehicle titles, and accessing online account passwords. We spent hours talking about my children, my fears, regrets, memories, joy, and sadness. We wondered why people don't plan better for the inevitable, leaving emotional decisions, such as burial versus cremation or casket selection, to the bereaved.

Yet, seventy-six days later, she was no more prepared than I to have her husband, John, succumb to a heart attack mere inches from his treadmill. What are we to make of this surreal situation? Together, we have six children between sixteen and twenty-eight; young people who matured light years in the cessation of a heart-beat, having lost the two gregarious men who weaved in and out of each other's lives for more than two decades.

Ted and John stood up for each other, first at John's wedding, finally at Ted's funeral. Beginning in the eighties, they whetted their political appetites over martinis and meals in our dining rooms, often boring their wives but always entertaining each other. Yet, they are gone, resting a wingspan from each other in a cemetery close to the neighborhood in which they spent most of their adult lives.

In roughly the same period, an earthquake in Haiti rendered thousands of other women widows, and children fatherless. News reports of the events are horrific to watch but, absent a personal connection, render one a voyeur of another's grief.

Ted and Johnny's deaths have caused a tsunami in relatively small Mendota Heights, Minnesota, where our daughters attend a small all-girl high school together, and in the larger legal community where they both practiced for decades. We expect some fatalities to occur, in combat or on the freeway. We do not anticipate that seemingly healthy hearts will fail and prevent our loved ones from returning home at night. When two men oft described as "larger than life" die in their fifties—before or after exercising—the impact sends shockwaves. Our faith is rattled. Questions plague us. Consequently, scores of women are turning to husbands who hold high-stress jobs, imploring them to get a physical, cut back at work, get their affairs in order. Our children's peers are wondering if their dad will be next.

We are now proprietors of our own grief. While Ann, our children, and I are tethered forever by our tragic losses, we are also buoyed by the love and kindness of others who share our heartache and confusion about this sequence of events. Many can imagine our guys "working the room" together in paradise, kibitzing about politics, the Minnesota Twins, or the Rolling Stones, elbowing each other to be the first to chat with Ronald Reagan. Yet those musings provide meager comfort from thoughts about the "big moments" on the horizon. It is incomprehensible that we will go through graduations, weddings, and welcome grandchildren without our men.

As parents, it is difficult to know whether our kids pay attention to our lectures or take note of behaviors we try to model for them. The eulogies by Dan Sullivan, twenty-five, and Will McDonald, nineteen, left no doubt that these sons had been listening, watching, and learning.

Two days before his twenty-fifth birthday, Dan observed about Ted:

> *In a world where many are content to just be, my father wanted to BE everything. Whether he was part of the pit crew at an Indy car race, sailing the Apostle Islands, bone fishing in the Keys, or opening the door to the law practice he loved, he made it count, and he did it with faith."*

He shared three lessons he learned from his dad:

> *First, it is un-American to drive by a child's lemonade stand and not buy a glass. A strong work ethic, the stomach to take a chance, and a little moxie could take a person a long way in life.*
> *Second, you can learn a lot about a man and how he*

will conduct his business with you by the way he treats his spouse. In this regard, my dad was loving, incredibly generous, thoughtful, understanding, and lucky.

Lastly, always spend the money on a nice pair of shoes.

Dad, today I am wearing a pair of yours. Black Cole Haan, size eleven. They are too big for me right now, but I hope to grow into them.

Will said of John:

I learned more from my father in a single car ride to our favorite restaurant, Davanni's, than I ever did from any textbook or classroom. He taught me how to walk and to talk, how to dance and to sing, how to laugh and to celebrate, how to cry and to grieve, how to think and to study, and how to embrace life's gifts and tragedies. He taught me the value of a strong work ethic, and the rewards and respect from others that comes with having it. He taught me that life isn't worth living if you can't enjoy it. He taught me how to be a son, a brother, a husband, and a father. He taught me how to cheer and to mourn, how to love and to NEVER hate. He was my ultimate teacher, and to put it simply, he taught me how to live.

We may never understand these unexpected deaths or be prepared for others to come. But Dan and Will confirmed that, while we cannot spare them from heartache, we can provide our children with a roadmap to a life well lived.

Survivor Guilt

WE NEED LIFE TO MAKE SENSE. When tragedy strikes, we seek answers. Yet, brooding can foster crippling emotions, such as angst, fear, and bitterness. It can spurn confusion, and even paralysis.

Guilt can be equally destructive.

After Ted's heart attack, I wondered why I lived through my cancer battle, but he died in an emergency room with no loved ones by his side. He had such reverence for life. While he viewed the glass as half full, I often saw it as half empty. Most of all, I believed he was more lovable, loving, and loved. Why him, instead of me?

In moments of clarity, I scolded myself for such ruminations. Ted would have been annoyed by thoughts like *it should have been me*. Rather, he would have felt his life was of greater consequence if those of us who survived him recognized how fleeting life can be. He would have been honored if his death motivated others to become more compassionate or charitable while they could. He would have expected me to set the proper example for our children, who were reeling from his death.

As long as our hearts are beating, we have a measure, at least, of free will. Free will empowers us to control our choices, attitudes, and behavior in the aftermath of the unimaginable. By exercising free will we elect not to be victims.

Father Johnson's reminder, that we can choose to become bitter or better, provided a valuable framework within which I could measure my thoughts and actions. I knew it would take little effort to become bitter. I could try to eat or drink away my pain. Rather than assuaging the guilt, though, such indulgences would surely fuel it, and breed new problems. Moreover, my children would be watching. I would not let them down.

On the other hand, choosing better would require extraordinary effort when energy was in short supply. Choosing better required me to rise after a sleepless night, slap on lipstick or a hat, and meet a friend for coffee, rather than stay in bed to watch crime show reruns.

Choosing better meant I had to abandon the questions for which there were no satisfactory answers.

Choosing better required me to stop the negative thoughts and look at the glass as half full.

Choosing better wouldn't mean the pain and longing would miraculously disappear, the questions would cease, or the shattered dreams would be restored. But choosing better meant survivor's guilt would have to find a new host.

Fish Out of Water

IN JUNE OF 2010, Jack spent a week in northern Minnesota at an Autism Society of Minnesota camp. It was a four-hour drive each way. Rather than drive up and back in one day, I decided to spend a little time regrouping and relaxing "up north," as we say in Minnesota.

I found a peaceful and pristine family-run resort outside of Park Rapids, near Itasca State Park. The timing wasn't optimal. It was Jack's nineteenth birthday, and the first Father's Day after Ted's death. My heart ached for our kids. I was lonely. But the resort was lovely and a great place to write.

I returned to Half Moon Trail the following summer for a longer stretch, which turned out to be a time of peace and discomfort, rumination, and revelation. My getaway inspired a reflective column.

* * *

In three decades as a relocated Minnesotan, I typically haven't spent more than a few days at a time vacationing in the state. With my son tucked away at a nearby summer camp for kids with autism, I decided it was time to enjoy a part of the state I'd never visited. I located a family resort online that met my criteria—clean, safe, and affordable.

When I entered the cozy lakeside cabin, the silence gripped me unexpectedly. I was unaccustomed to quiet so palpable it grazed my fingertips. Realizing the room had no TV, I felt a twinge of panic, for I end every day with its chatter in the background. Gradually, my mind adjusted to the quiet, much as eyes adapt to sudden darkness. Yet I never found comfort in it.

Throughout my getaway, two thoughts poked away at me like the woodpecker on a tree outside my cabin. Become one with nature. Live in the moment. I'd packed these sentiments, shared by others, along with my clothing, books, and toiletries. But they were buried under a stream of mental traffic involving weighty and trivial concerns alike. They proved difficult to honor, as I remained bound to home through my mobile phone.

As I marked the eighteenth month since I'd suddenly lost my spouse, the device distracted me from a discomforting awareness: I was a spectator at a family centered resort—a fish out of water, so to speak.

It's impossible to either become one with nature or to live in the moment with an ever-dinging device in one's pocket. Yet, I was unable—or unwilling—to part with it for long. Like the TV shows that offered background noise and companionship, the mobile phone became my lifeline to others. Talking and texting became the unbidden strategies that kept the void in my life at bay.

Important medical appointments for my son Jack vied for attention with the cries of a loon and the elegance of a rare Lady Slipper wildflower on the shoreline. Becoming one with nature, I concluded, does not just happen. I'd failed to prepare so I would be able to ease out of one world and into another.

Weeklong vacations were rare during our twenty years of marriage. There were always barriers to extended getaways: Ted's demanding job, the challenges of vacationing with a special needs child, negotiating time away with the older kids in our blended family, relentless health issues. Many friends spent much of the summer at their cabins. How did they manage their mail, or care for one household, while they were vacationing at another?

In the days I spent alone at the lake, it was often tough to venture from my cabin. Evidence of what my family had missed out on was inescapable. Rain or shine, adults cast their lines with their kids, guests from every generation played billiards and badminton, and grandkids roasted marshmallows for grandparents over a blazing fire. Others didn't appear to be tethered to their phones or worried about Internet access. They were listening to the loons and the laughter of young children with an ease that should accompany a week's respite from life back home.

To my eye, other guests had discovered the splendor of northern Minnesota, and figured out how to overcome the obstacles in their own lives so they could enjoy it year after year. They were living in the moment. They were collecting memories made of fishing lines and worms, and paddle boats and ping pong competitions they might later recall as some of their best moments together. Family vacations are not utopian, but they are vacations, after all. Years from now, no one will recall how, as kids, they were texting or tweeting their friends, or their parents were checking their email and paying their bills online.

Life will go on, as it always has, and as it should. With two weddings on the horizon, my family will soon stretch without the man who spoke often of memory-building moments.

Although, at times, I am shackled by regrets of what we didn't experience while Ted was with us, I'm hopeful we can become one of those multi-generational families who make the annual trek up north. I want my kids and their kids to appreciate that the loon's call, the sparkle of the lake in the morning, and a walk through a rain-dampened forest are more memorable than the ding of an electronic device announcing the arrival of yet another email.

Do You Regret Having Me?

WHEN JACK WAS IN MIDDLE SCHOOL, we went to Wisconsin to celebrate Grandma Sullivan's birthday. As we sat outside enjoying our burgers and brats, Grandma began to ask Jack questions.

"How is school? What are you up to these days?"

He cut her off. "Grandma, you know I don't like idle chitchat."

Indeed, he prefers to speak when the mood strikes him. Years later, the mood struck as we were driving to the grocery store.

"Do you regret having me?" he asked. He knew I loved him, he said, but felt responsible for me quitting my job as a lawyer when he was diagnosed with autism.

I responded quickly, hoping to squelch his festering doubts.

"I have no regrets," I said. "In fact, I am a better person because of you."

He insisted he hadn't asked because of something I'd said or done. I was unconvinced. I suspected he'd figured out that I (and others) spent much of his young life trying to fix him. I imagine his concern emanated from a lifetime of seeing or hearing he is different; that some of his behavior is socially unacceptable for reasons he may not—or may—comprehend.

People who are born with challenges are labeled "disabled," implying they don't measure up. Yet, Jack has overcome many hurdles to accomplish tasks that are simple for many, but considerable for him. He moved into an apartment by himself when he was eighteen years old. He's learned how to plan, shop, and prepare his meals; launder his clothes; and clean his apartment. How many young men do that so early in life?

He is also the most sensitive person I know. I'm often struck by the irony. I worried so much about how Jack would deal with Ted's death. Yet, of the four kids, he is the one who most often mentions their dad to me. He's the one to remind me of Ted's absence on holidays or birthdays.

With the fifth anniversary of Ted's death approaching, Jack spoke openly about his grief. He began by reminding me that December 15 was on the horizon; then his voice would fade, as he looked at me, waiting for *me* to fill in the words *he* still has such difficulty saying aloud after five years.

He surprised (and distressed) me by disclosing his fear of losing me. He reminded me he had almost lost me twice—when I had cancer and when I was in a car accident. Who knew he recalled those events after so many years?

It's not easy for one parent to bear the load that once was borne by two. What is the sole surviving parent to say? I acknowledged the truth—I will die someday—and assured Jack he would be cared for when that day comes. He politely thanked me, but circled back to his principal concern: he would miss me.

Jack loves babies, dogs, and cats, and always roots for the underdog. He ends every phone conversation with a heartfelt "I love you." He donated his bone marrow to his sister without ever asking how it might affect him. He is thoughtful and bright and creative. How could I regret having him?

Choosing Hope

MY SISTER TRACI and I began smoking as teenagers. I didn't indulge for long. I didn't like the taste or the smell, and knew I was only lighting up to fit in with the other kids who were smoking. Traci liked it more; like my mom, she spent years lighting up. I hated the habit and couldn't help but wonder how great a role it played in my parents' health histories. Mom smoked until she could not hold her cigarette, and I had a hard time forgiving her for it.

Over the years, Traci's smoking was the source of many arguments between us. I wanted to be empathetic when she said she was trying to quit, but I couldn't understand her choice, or her struggle. I thought about how both our parents smoked and died of cancer before they were fifty; how I'd dodged cancer in my forties. Was it a stretch to fear that cancer was waiting in the shadows for Traci, too? The thought plagued me; I didn't want to lose my only sister, too.

Traci stopped smoking in 2014. She didn't stop because I hounded her, or because she had cancer. She stopped because she was diagnosed with a fairly rare, degenerative disease.

Dystonia is characterized by involuntary muscle contractions that cause abnormal postures or involuntary repetitive movements ranging from twitching to spasms so intense they can catapult a person from her bed. Dystonia does not affect a person's cognitive abilities or personality.

I learned that a young woman in my writer's group also had dystonia. I invited Traci to come from Tampa, Florida, to Minnesota to meet Nikki Abramson and to attend a local women's conference. Nikki and I were two of five panel members who would speak at the conference about dealing with challenges.

Because it only affects about 300,000 Americans, dystonia is frequently misdiagnosed or undiagnosed. In the fall of 2013, Traci told her internist she had head tremors. The doctor ordered blood tests but never followed up with her. A year later, a physician's assistant noticed the tremors. Suspecting Parkinson's, he referred her to a neurologist, who diagnosed focal dystonia.

Nikki's health challenges began at birth, when she failed to thrive. When she was six years old, a doctor said she would likely die in her teens from mitochondrial myopathy, a rare disease that causes muscle weakness throughout her body. Defying the prediction, Nikki powered through scoliosis and severe allergies. Frequently ill, but always determined, she completed high school and earned a teaching degree at Bethel University in St. Paul, Minnesota.

In August 2010, Nikki was involved in an automobile accident that caused severe pain and what she believed to be seizures. A chiropractor diagnosed generalized dystonia (meaning it affects all, or most, of the body) and referred her to a neurologist who confirmed the diagnosis and prescribed Botox treatments and physical therapy.

Instead of launching the teaching career she'd dreamed of, Nikki became homebound. Pain, fatigue, and muscle spasms transformed her from a high-energy extrovert to a lonely introvert. Old friends slipped away, replaced by new ones, typically older adults with stories of their own.

Nikki needs assistance with showering, combing her hair, and applying makeup. Her head lists to the right, and she struggles to walk straight, if at all. She relies on a wheelchair to travel distances others can easily walk. Given her limited range of motion, it is hard for her to drive. She limits her driving to a short distance from home. On a good day, she has three to four hours of energy.

Traci experiences excruciating headaches that start at the

base of her neck and radiate up the back of her head. At times her head shakes from side to side as if she is expressing disagreement, though she is just listening. Preparing dinner can be exhausting. She has difficulty swallowing. Her feet are often numb. Her hands shake. Her handwriting is illegible.

Experts say many people who live with dystonia become dependent, isolated, lonely, and depressed. Nikki quickly helped Traci to feel less alone and better informed. She shared resources with her. They text and connect on Facebook.

Traci and Nikki were born decades apart, hold dissimilar political views, and reside in different parts of the country. Yet their common struggle trumps their differences.

Traci, an optimist by nature, vacillates between accepting her life is irrevocably changed and thinking it's not that bad. She can barely look at photos of people her doctor described as "pretzels." I don't want to look like that," she says of people whose heads rest on their shoulders, frozen in place. "As much pain as I'm in now, that looks horrendous."

Both women have learned to be advocates. Traci doesn't know whether it would have made a difference if her doctor had detected the condition earlier; but she's confident that if the physician's assistant hadn't diagnosed her, she would be thinking it was something in her head, instead of dystonia. She encourages others to seek medical help if they suspect a problem. Otherwise, they might question whether their imagination is playing games with them.

As Nikki's peers are launching careers and families, she is considering where she will live if her parents retire and relocate to another state. Who will care for her, as her mother does now? How will she support herself?

Similarly, Traci, a self-employed realtor in Tampa, is anticipating her challenges and exploring changes she and her husband Charlie may need to make, particularly if she can no longer drive.

●

As a writer and speaker, Nikki shares her story to encourage others. In her memoir, *I Choose Hope: Overcoming Challenges with Faith and Positivity*, she writes, "Hope is all around us. We need to look for it, grab a hold of it, and not let it go. We need to feel what hope feels like, so when we lose hope we can grab it again. We need people around us to encourage us when we can't seem to find our way. If we all continued to press on and be hopeful, we would live a much happier life."

Care for the Caregivers

WE KNOW THEM. We are them. The bone-tired folks who change their parents' Depends, sit with children through chemotherapy, and answer the same question from an aging spouse over and over and over.

Unpaid caregivers often step in after learning a loved one has dementia, cerebral palsy, mental illness, addiction, or a brain injury. The list is endless. Caregivers provide emotional and financial support, and assist with personal hygiene.

The duties take a toll, spurring emotional, mental, and physical health problems. Depression is common. Drug and alcohol use often increase. Healthy eating, sleep, exercise, and socializing are cast aside. Anxiety ramps up, while self-esteem declines. Finances are strained.

Caregiving is not just a burden, though. It can be very gratifying. Minnesota author and speaker Molly Cox didn't choose to become her parents' caregiver; she accepted a calling that lasted ten years. She nursed her mother during her battle with cancer, and took on the primary caregiver role for her father, who had Alzheimer's disease.

Caregiving was her honor, though she wouldn't have said that at the start. Juggling speaking, writing, and raising two kids was exhausting. Add another full-time job that entailed psychological stress and unchartered territory . . . the result was an ever-present feeling that no matter what you're doing, you should be doing something else. Molly came to realize that caregiving has limitations. And radical self-care is paramount.

"When you are dealing with a dementia patient, you may be getting calls five, six times a day. There comes a point where you know your life, as you knew it, is over. I can't imagine how a single mother can possibly care for aging parents and hold a job where she can't make phone calls or take a half-day without losing pay. And yet, that occurs every day.

Whether you are taking care of your mother, a special needs child, or a spouse, everyone has the same experience and a common response. If you ring that bell one more time . . . if you ask me to do one more thing . . . Everyone experiences it. Only half of the people talk about it."

Even the happiest people can become exhausted under the weight of overwhelming demands. An expert on stress management, life balance, and humor, Molly prescribes regular doses of laughter.

"People rub off on you—good or bad. Are you with energy suckers, or are you with people who support you, lift you up, and make you laugh? When you lose your smile, your ability to laugh, it's time to get serious about the lighter side of life."

I've spent much of my adult life in a caregiving role. I have also watched many friends care for ailing parents, spouses, and children. Caring for someone in need is both exhausting and rewarding. I regret I didn't meet Molly Cox sooner. I could have used more laughter in my life.

Survivor With a Smile

THE MONTHS AFTER TED DIED were unpredictable and erratic. I greeted some days with energy and enthusiasm. I went through many of the motions of life feeling like a zombie sporting a splash of lipstick. Sometimes it seemed I merely ripped the day off of the calendar, as my son Jack did for so many years. He'd begin each day by reading the joke on his Homer Simpson daily calendar. Then he would tear it off, toss it in the pile, and go about his business.

I wasn't the only one to muddle through 2010. It seemed everyone had something sapping energy, emotions, time, and bank accounts. Middle age has a wide wingspan. Parents, spouses, children, and friends . . . when you're in the middle of your life, you never know who will face a new challenge.

Too proud to ask for help, but not to accept it, I welcomed everything that kept us afloat. Early on, it was the steady supply of meals, for I had little energy to shop, cook, and wash dishes.

I appreciated text messages, cards, calls, and emails from family and friends offering positive thoughts and prayers. Encouraging words, typically, "You are so strong," buoyed me. I could believe in myself if others believed in me.

Though preparing meals was a challenge, it paled in comparison to the pile of paperwork that demanded my attention. Who knew how exhausting it would be to file for Social Security benefits or change titles to cars and a home?

As I anticipated the first anniversary of Ted's death, I had moments of gripping anxiety. Thinking about the phone conversation with the emergency room doctor I never met, I had to force myself to breathe. Remembering with equal measure of clarity and confusion the events that followed, I felt as though I'd witnessed the unfolding of another's nightmare. Yet, it was mine.

As my first year as a widow and single mom came to an end, I was reflective about where I'd been, where I was headed, and how I would get there. I'd heard that the second year after a death is harder than the first. How would I continue to roll out of bed and tear the pages off of a new calendar? I imagined my constellation of support: my kids, strong and resilient; my family and friends, especially Ann, my sister in sorrow, who shared my crazy journey. I hoped I could muster energy to enjoy exercise, music, and laughter, and to continue with the writing that had been so therapeutic.

I pictured the angels who had lifted me up so I could make it through the first, numbing year. I hoped they knew who they were, for I cherished them all. I promised that if they kept the support coming, my crew and I would not only survive, we would thrive. And I promised that when their time came, as it inevitably would, I would pay it forward.

A Servant's Heart

MANY OF MY FRIENDS are Minnesota natives who have the extended families I've yearned for. Their siblings live moments away; cousins attend school and church together. Their parents attend grandparents' day at their kids' schools and are active in their lives.

My friends Rick and Tricia Long are a prime example. During the years they lived across the street with their three sons, I would watch enviously as Rick's dad pulled up to their home in his big Cadillac. Dick Long had the type of relationship with his grandchildren I longed for my children to have.

Dick's was the classic rags-to-riches tale. He was born in Chicago in 1929. His older brother died when he was eleven. Shortly thereafter, his forty-two-year-old father dropped dead from a heart attack. His mother had four young children and few marketable skills, so at age thirteen, Dick quit school and went to work. He wanted to ensure his family kept their home and his younger siblings remained in school.

Dick worked several jobs at once. He wrapped asbestos around the inner shell of water heaters, working in ninety-degree heat with no air conditioning. He changed oil on automobiles in the grease pit. He raised chickens so he could sell the eggs on a street corner at night, after working one or two day jobs.

He never finished high school or attended college, but he was a voracious reader and an astute learner. He briefly worked as a policeman before his brother enticed him into the automobile business. Eventually he landed in St. Paul, where he lived with his wife and six children. While Dick built Long Cadillac, Mary ran the household and managed the kids.

After Mary died in 1990, Dick shifted gears. The man whose business often kept him away from home sold the dealership and engaged with the family that included nineteen grandchildren and two great-grandchildren. He gave his children respite from parenting, taking the grandkids to his cabin to fish and share stories—but only after they were out of diapers. Not a modern man, Pops had his limits.

He also had his demons. An alcoholic, he had an affinity for those who shared the addiction for which he went through treatment and recovery multiple times. He was frequently seen sharing coffee, and an ear, when someone was down.

Although he was weary of battling significant health issues at the end of his life, he never lost his faith or optimism. When Dick said his final good-byes to his family, he was ready to be reunited with his beloved wife and to meet Jesus.

When Dick died days before Thanksgiving 2010, he left an impressive legacy, as evidenced by his son Rick's eulogy.

He has every civic recognition this city awards, but if you knew my dad, this is not what he would want to be remembered by. He would want to be known as a man who loved his family first, as a man who invested in friendships and people, and as a person who tirelessly gave back. My dad's true passion and mission in life was to assist the needy and to abolish hunger and homelessness . . . .

He often told us that if it weren't for a few lucky breaks, we all could be in the same position and would want someone there for us. My dad worked tirelessly on this mission. He was deeply involved with Catholic Charities, Loaves and Fishes, the Dorothy Day Center, as well as countless other charities and programs. It wasn't his leadership in this area that he would want to be remembered for, but the work he did and the difference he made."

Father John Malone of St. Paul was Dick's closest friend and confidant. To his mind, what really drove Dick was a deep religious faith, which found its expression in what he did and why he did it. Father Malone observed that while Dick's childhood was tough, it was nothing compared to that of many people Dick met at the Dorothy Day Center, where, for decades, thousands have received medical care, mental health services, shelter, showers, and holiday meals.

Dick's experiences added passion to what he did, but that was only half of the story. Dick also believed that you serve Christ by serving other people. He often did so by reaching out to those who no one else wanted to care for.

When tragedy crossed my threshold, a cohort of people followed, arms outstretched. They were (and continue to be) the Dick Longs in my life. I saw in their eyes, and heard in their voices, how much they wanted to help. Often too proud to ask for help, I saw their relief when I accepted offers to bring meals, plow my driveway, and mow my lawn.

Many understood intuitively when I was in need of a boost, sending "How's it going over there?" emails or "thinking of you" texts. I bear witness to the impact others make through gestures small and large. I will forever be grateful for those who not only reached out to me in the midst of their busy lives, but also taught me how to be a true friend in a time of need.

Fall in Love, Stay in Love

IN 1981 Sheila Delaney was one of just a few Minnesotans attending Boston College. On a fall day she was standing in the cafeteria line when an older man greeted her. Sheila had no idea that Bill Neenan was a man of the cloth, because he wasn't wearing a collar. As they chatted, the Iowa native was delighted to learn Sheila was from Minnesota.

Learning that Father Neenan was going on a retreat in the Midwest, Sheila invited him to visit her family at their summer home. That visit led to another, and another, until the Jesuit priest was embedded in the Delaney clan. Father Neenan spent Christmas with his adopted family in Minnesota. He performed marriage ceremonies for Sheila and her three sisters. Warmer days meant visits to the family's restful abode on the Wisconsin side of the river that separated it from Minnesota. Father Neenan said Mass, shared meals, and discussed books with Sheila's parents, contemporaries with whom he established a deep friendship.

As the years went by, Sheila engaged Father Neenan in spirited debates about religion. Without making excuses, he reminded her that the Catholic faith has been around for 2,000 years; that the church has always had organizational strife; that while the church and hierarchy have gone through horrible periods, the faith has never changed. The Jesuit approach to Catholicism—"You were born with gifts and it's your responsibility to make the most of them"—gave her new insight into an old institution and helped her to embrace her faith.

Father Neenan had a motto: "Fall in love, stay in love, and the rest will take care of itself." It applied to a host of situations.

"I think that is also what he was saying to me about the Catholic Church," Sheila said. "All this noise is bad. It's disheartening…but if you have fallen in love with the faith, with Jesus, with being part of this faith community, and you can find a way to stay in love with it, all this other stuff will sort itself out."

While she was still living in Boston, Sheila faced a difficult decision—whether to marry a New Englander who didn't share her desire to live in Minnesota. She turned to her mentor, and he offered her a useful approach to resolving dilemmas. If you have a difficult choice to make, he said, try to visualize yourself at the end of your life and imagine how it would feel if you chose Path A or Path B. The exercise was useful. Not able to imagine herself without him, Sheila married John Moroney and they remained in Boston until he received a job offer he couldn't refuse—in Minnesota.

The casual chat in a college cafeteria would never have occurred had Father Neenan not been charming and engaging, and Sheila open to meeting someone new. By looking up and being present, she, and three generations of her family, formed a rare friendship, filled with meaningful conversations and treasured memories. I can't help but wonder how often those chance encounters are lost, when our eyes are frequently downcast, focused on electronic devices, with little awareness of what is going on around us.

It's not that difficult. But how often do we allow ourselves the time to make new acquaintances? By simply stepping away from the wall, extending a hand, and making an introduction, we can open ourselves up to amazing friendships and opportunities.

How Much Is Enough?

I HAD PROMISED JULIA that I would keep our house until she completed her first year of college. She wanted a familiar home to return to. Having lost my family home when I was about her age, I completely understood.

After twenty-three years in the same home, I recognized when my neighbors were coming or going by the sound of their car engines. I looked forward to the spontaneous invitations from the Lanphers to throw on a swimsuit and head over for cocktails and conversation in the pool. I adored the twin boys across the street, as well as the ones who lived two houses down. It saddens me that I won't see them grow up and pose for prom pictures, or take the car for a spin for the first time.

But the five-bedroom house and yard were depleting my time, energy, and money. I was holding my breath for the day when the washer or dryer would go for a final spin, and I'd need to replace them. So when a purportedly eager buyer made an unsolicited and attractive cash offer for the house to see if I would bite, I did.

I quickly held a garage sale, never expecting that the home sale would fall through (as did two others), and that I wouldn't move until the following spring. In retrospect, the time, energy, and money spent unloading the house prepared me emotionally to move to a brand new home in a nearby community.

When the moving vans finally arrived in April 2013, I was exhausted from more than sixty showings, a dozen open houses, and three unsuccessful offers. The only silver lining was my realtor, Julie Gould, who demonstrated that a good realtor is also part therapist. The experience was also good fodder for another column.

. . .

The "for sale" sign staked in my front yard is among the first as my baby boomer neighbors also begin to grapple with questions about "how much." How much space do we need now that we've launched our offspring? How much stuff is enough? How much do we want to spend on housing for one or two, as opposed to a handful? How much do we value things we would have to pay to store or transport? These are personal decisions, informed by values, needs, and financial means.

For the past twenty-three years, I have opened the same door each morning to retrieve the newspaper from the porch step. As I pore through the closets, garage, storage room, and file cabinets, I am reminded of how each of my family members spent their time. We collected Pokémon cards and Beanie Babies. Wine glasses and coffee mugs. Tennis racquets and camping gear. Halloween costumes and holiday decorations. Books and bikes. Medical records and surgical scars. Frequent flier miles and consumer debt. Diplomas and death certificates.

But I encounter the most important things all around me. They are not found in closets or boxes, though they are often triggered by the tangible things, and especially by photographs. They are the memories.

In the early 1990s, the adults on my block gathered in front of our suburban homes as our kids drove Barbie jeeps and rode Big Wheels, barefoot and helmetless. We formed friendships over beers as together we learned the unscripted art of parenting. As the kids grew older, we saw less of the adults and more of the kids. By the time they were in high school, I could guesstimate how many boys and girls had gathered in the basement from the size, style, and number of boots, flip-flops, or smelly tennis shoes piled in the entryway, depending on the season.

As I wander through our home, I see an endless array of things: shoes, handbags, fishing bobbers, golf clubs, drill bits, screwdrivers, phone chargers, TV sets, and lawn chairs. Without the people with whom I shared them, I find there are surprisingly few things I cherish. They include the fondue pots around which a dozen girls sat for hours dipping their sticks, first in cheese, then in chocolate; the jigsaw puzzles we collectively solved while the Thanksgiving turkey was browning in its juice; the Christmas stockings I decorated for each family member and hung in the same location each year.

Many of my favorite things aged in the keepsake boxes I started for each family member years ago. I'd forgotten about the Mother's Day cards that brought both tears and smiles. With fresh eyes, I imagine little fingers reaching into the crayon box to select just the right combination of colors to write the words that rarely passed over lips, but were more readily shared in a card.

But it was time spent together that I treasure most of all. The cut-throat games of Catch Phrase, wine-fueled political debates with friends who preferred donkeys to our elephants, karaoke parties, Easter egg hunts, and Christmas caroling with neighbors.

Looking out my window, I see a life cycle in action. New neighbors are becoming acquainted as their kids ride past on bikes, shoes on their feet and helmets on their heads, reflecting a heightened state of vigilance. It won't be long before those children have their own cellphones and their parents no longer have a landline.

As they assume mortgages and birth their own babies, will my kids be consumers or savers? Decades from now, will they feel satisfied or regretful about how they used their resources? Will they feel they struck the proper balance between time and things? Will they have gathered more memories or mementos?

Bret Baier's Quandary

BRET BAIER HAS MADE A CAREER of reporting other peoples' stories. In 2007 the evening anchor of *Fox News Channel's Special Report with Bret Baier* had what he described as an idyllic life. He had a beautiful wife, and a child on the way.

When their son Paul was born, the Baier family reveled in their joy—for one day. On the second day, Dr. Gerard Martin shared shocking news: their six-pound, twelve-ounce baby had five congenital heart defects.

The cardiologist explained that, while heart disease can be simple, Paul's was complex. Within the next two weeks he would need surgery on a heart that was structurally very complicated. Without the surgery, he would die. Even if he survived he would have ongoing issues with his heart.

Dr. Richard Jonas is a world-renowned pediatric cardiac surgeon, and head of cardiology at Children's Hospital in Washington, DC. He has a successful track record of performing the surgery that Paul required. But Dr. Jonas was out of the country and couldn't expedite his return to operate on Paul.

Their heads spinning from the unexpected news, Bret and Amy debated whether to wait for Dr. Jonas to return in ten days or transfer Paul to another hospital for immediate surgery.

Struggling to choose between expediency and expertise, they sought guidance. Though they peppered Paul's new team of doctors with questions, they received noncommittal responses, such as

"Can't really say." Frustrated, Bret recognized it was the defensive strategy of malpractice-phobic doctors.

Ultimately, the man who has interviewed United States presidents found the right words: "What would you do if it were your child?" Without hesitation, three physicians offered their personal opinions. They would wait for Dr. Jonas.

Bret and Amy indulged questions, anger, and second-guessing for a while. Then they agreed to cast aside negative thoughts, to remain positive and faithful. They decided Amy would nurture Paul, while Bret handled the medical questions and communications with family, friends, and colleagues. They made a pact to exchange a high-five at the end of each day and to repeat their mantra: "We are one day closer to getting Paul home."

Paul's condition is so complicated few children survive it. Yet, he did; though he underwent three open-heart surgeries, seven angioplasties, and an unrelated stomach surgery in the first seven years of his life. The high-energy boy with the prominent scar on his chest will require additional intervention. Until then, he lives life with vigor, playing soccer and taking golf lessons with his younger brother.

In 2014, Bret published *Special Heart: A Journey of Faith, Hope, Courage and Love.* It is a personal account of how the Baiers faced their challenge with faith and support. They donate all proceeds of *Special Heart* sales to promising congenital heart disease research and treatments around the country. They hope the research will lead to less intrusive, and less painful procedures for Paul and thousands like him.

In addition to sharing their story, they've become advocates for the 36,000 children born with heart disease each year. Bret and Amy are active at Children's Hospital, where Dr. Jonas continues to treat Paul. The couple has logged many hours in the children's hospital waiting room alongside parents from disparate cultures. They've experienced an interesting phenomenon. As anxious parents await news of their children's condition, divisive issues such as politics, religion, and world views cede to fears, hope, and shared dialogue about what is happening with their child and what will make him well. Though he reports on what is happening at the highest level of government in the United States and abroad, Bret now does so with the insight that comes from living through a personal hell. Each night, as he assumes the anchor chair, he is mindful that many families deal with much weightier concerns than what one Democrat or Republican says about another.

Vince Flynn: Keep the Faith

MY BOOKCASE holds every one of Vince Flynn's novels featuring a fictional CIA counterterrorism operative, Mitch Rapp, as tenacious as the man who created him. Every fall, Ted, Dan, and I waited eagerly for his latest novel to be released, for we all enjoyed a good page-turner.

But there was something else about the St. Paul author I found compelling. Though he received more than sixty rejections by publishers, he didn't abandon his dream. He self-published his first novel, *Term Limits*, in 1997, then secured a lasting relationship with publisher Simon & Schuster.

As a fan and a writer, I was eager to meet the author who lived minutes from our home, and with whom we shared many friends. But as the mother of a son with autism, I was interested in meeting the author who despite, or because of, his dyslexia, had become an international success.

One spring morning in 2010, our paths crossed at St. Thomas Academy, the high school both Vince and Dan graduated from. At my behest, a mutual friend introduced us. Literally cornered by me, Vince was too gracious to refuse my request for an interview.

On a sunny April afternoon in 2010, we met at a coffee shop in Mendota Heights, the small suburb of St. Paul I called home. When Vince stepped out of his vehicle, sunglasses obscuring his eyes, I fought back a chuckle. Of course a guy who wrote about fighting terrorists would drive a black Range Rover with tinted windows.

We began to chat, and I immediately sensed I had pulled him away from work on his latest novel. "Yes," he said, "I had." But he'd heard that Ted and John had died a few months earlier. Echoing one of my favorite sentiments (everything in life is relative), he said that leaving his writing to meet me was a minor disruption in a life that was going well for him.

In the hour that followed, we engaged in an unexpectedly personal conversation before he dashed off to pick up his daughters at school. He spoke of trying to maintain a normal life as the father of three, and how difficult it was to strike a balance between his public success and the privacy his family coveted. But his life was good, and he felt blessed. His one regret, he said, was that he had not met his wife Lysa sooner. She was truly the love of his life.

Vince spoke candidly about his school days. He had been an average student because his brain played tricks on him. He would see the word "dab" where most readers would see "bad." Just the prospect of reading aloud in front of classmates sent him into a cold sweat. He couldn't put the words in the right sequence. Math presented similar challenges. He understood concepts but jumbled numbers. By grade three, specialists said he had dyslexia, a condition affecting about twenty percent of us.

Growing up, he didn't talk about his dyslexia. But his secret unraveled in college when a theology professor gave him an "F" on a paper and expressed doubts about him graduating. He learned that basketball star Al McGuire had overcome his dyslexia by revisiting reading and writing fundamentals. If it worked for Al, it could work for him.

He became a prolific reader. He particularly enjoyed Robert Ludlum, Dick Francis, and Leon Uris novels. In his twenties, he decided to write a book.

Vince came to view his dyslexia as a gift. He credited it with giving him amazing situational awareness and great instincts. He was able to see patterns where others saw chaos. Empathetic toward students who also had dyslexia, he frequently visited with them at area schools. He encouraged students to face their fears and deal with them. But he also challenged them to find their gifts, whether in sports, art, music, or stamp collecting. "When kids know they are good at one thing they won't be as discouraged when they are bad at another," he said. He found self-worth and identity as an athlete. The writing came later.

When we met again in October 2010 to discuss his latest book, *American Assassin*, he surprised me by inquiring about my family, recalling details I assumed he would have forgotten. He spoke passionately about his respect for the men and women in the military and clandestine services, who featured so prominently in his novels. He abhorred political correctness and the hypocrisy of politicians who publicly condemned CIA practices, but privately condoned them.

A year later, Vince learned he was suffering from stage-three metastatic prostate cancer, a disease that commonly afflicts men over sixty-five. He was forty-five. Though he published a book each fall, his cancer treatment forced him to delay publication of *The Last Man* until February 2012, which is when we last spoke.

Though we had met at our regular coffee shop to discuss *The Last Man*, the conversation lingered on cancer, and life's challenges. He had recently completed his initial treatment and felt better than he had in years. Cancer had put the fear of God in him and caused him to focus on his mortality. He had his eye on the future—graduations and marriages and grandchildren. My eyes shared his focus, though I was struggling with experiencing those big moments without Ted.

Vince offered an interesting perspective on the power of words. His writing career had prepared him for his cancer battle, he said. To get published you have to overcome odds greater than beating cancer—and he had done that thirteen times. "Fighting cancer is like writing a book," he said. "It takes time. You can't wake up one morning and decide that you are going to be cancer free in a month. You just have to get up and put one foot in front of another, and put yourself in the best position to be cancer free. And you can't quit."

Before long, I heard through the grapevine that his cancer was back, and Vince was fighting it aggressively—and privately. Details were surprisingly scarce about a well-known guy in a town aptly known as "Saint Small." On June 19, my friend Julie sent a text: Vince had died during the night surrounded by family, close friends, and his priest.

Five days later, well over a thousand people filled the St. Paul Cathedral to say farewell to Vinnie. They spanned both the length and the breadth of his life, from childhood friends to politicians and celebrities. I didn't know Vince well and had only met Lysa a couple of times. Yet I attended the funeral because I knew how much it mattered to me when people from all quadrants of my family's lives came to honor Ted.

In his eulogy, Tom Tracy offered a glimpse into his close friend's final moments.

Even as it became clear that time was slipping away, Vince remained upbeat, gracious, and selfless. He never complained, despite profound pain and debilitating weakness. He was laser-focused on Lysa and the kids. He wanted them to know he loved them. He didn't want to be the center of attention. He didn't want anyone to worry about him. He wanted life to continue in its usual fashion around him.

Late last Tuesday, Vince's brother Tim called to say Vince's body was failing. It was hard to believe it had come to this, in light of Vince's steadfast determination and optimism. At the hospital, it was clear to all that Vince was at peace. His life-long faith in God gave him total confidence that Lysa, Dane, Ingrid, and Ana were safe in His hands. He was unafraid and ready to accept God's will. It was heartbreaking for all who were packed tightly around Vince's bed as their husband, father, son, brother, and friend took his last breath, but it was also exceedingly beautiful.

We are all so lucky to have known Vince Flynn. May we never forget his love, purity, strength, and compassion.

Vince had a mantra and it was with those words that Tom concluded a beautiful eulogy: *Always keep the faith.* Vince's life and death remind us that we have a choice. When editors reject our manuscripts; when our brains transpose letters and numbers; when we contract a terminal illness before age fifty, we have a choice. We can be bitter. Or we can be better.

A Three-Legged Walk

WHILE SOME PEOPLE may prefer to navigate life alone, my strength flows from solidarity. I appreciate having someone who understands my struggles as much as I enjoy lending an ear or a shoulder to another in need.

Though I visited autism support groups, I often left more fearful than I arrived, after listening to tearful stories from parents whose older kids wore diapers or couldn't say, "I love you." Instead, I have relied on my siblings and girlfriends for their patience, insight, and candor. We have burned up the phone lines and logged many miles walking and talking about life. Years before we both became members of the freakin' widows club, I had an eye-opening conversation with my friend Ann.

We were walking on a Florida beach in 2008 when the conversation turned to the challenges we faced in our respective households. I had angst about what the future held for Jack, then a teenager. She was worried about the future with her mother, who was in the early stages of dementia.

For years, I'd told Ann how Jack's impulsive behavior had kept me on edge in a way her typically developing children's behavior had not. Until that walk, I don't know that she was able to fully grasp what I'd dealt with. But as she talked about how variable her mother's behavior had become, how she went in and out of lucidity, and how she needed so much more care than before, we recognized the similarity in our challenges.

While Ann had new insight into my journey, I had a presentiment about hers. Long before it affected Ann's family, Alzheimer's made a stealthy entrance into my mother's side of the family. It struck my grandfather, stealing Grandpop's sharp mind, and his health. Mom was an only child, so my grandmother turned to my siblings and me (especially Traci, who lived closest to them) for support.

Although Traci provided regular updates about Grandpop's decline, I was totally unprepared when I visited him in the Florida nursing home where he spent his final days. My grandmother, who had seen him wither away, couldn't understand why I didn't recognize the unshaven little guy slumped in the wheelchair as Grandpop, just as he didn't recognize me as his eldest granddaughter. I'd gone to visit a big, strong man who was known for his bear hugs, jokes, and bellowing voice. Instead, I was greeted by an unrecognizable shadow. It was heartbreaking to see what had happened to him in the twilight of his life.

As Ann and I walked and talked, I thought about the saying that you can't really understand another's journey until you've walked in her shoes. Our experiences were not so similar that we were wearing the same pair of shoes that day. Rather, we were taking a three-legged walk, each with one foot in our own shoe and one foot in a shared shoe. As heavy as the conversation was, it felt good to finally have my struggles understood, as well as to empathize with what Ann was experiencing.

Our chat also underscored the intriguing parallels between autism and Alzheimer's. Although autism appears at daybreak and Alzheimer's at sunset, both conditions have a dramatic impact on families, who deal with embarrassing behaviors and awkward hygiene issues. Respecting one's dignity, while protecting him from dangers he may not appreciate, can be worrisome and challenging. Both conditions can involve complicated financial considerations, such as whether to care for the loved one at home, often at great expense, or to opt for a residential living option—an emotional and costly move, as well.

Both are a type of ambiguous loss. An autism diagnosis can shatter dreams of what life was expected to be. Alzheimer's transforms adult relationships; companionship slips away, replaced by the pain of helplessly watching a loved one's life unravel. Both conditions can require extraordinary sacrifices of family and friends, with little or none of the reciprocity inherent in most relationships.

Unburdening our hearts, trusting another to listen respectfully to our woes, is a vital lesson in the manual. Regardless of where on the spectrum our challenges fall, it's always easier to navigate them with a friend or loved one. We all need someone with strong shoulders and an empathetic heart. We all need a cherished friend who likes to take three-legged walks.

Lee Woodruff: In an Instant

LESS THAN TWO YEARS after I walked the beach with Ann, I met Lee Woodruff. Lee is an author, professional speaker, and broadcast news contributor. In the spirited blonde, I found a woman who epitomizes a survivor with a smile: bright, funny, and compassionate. Though I've only met her twice, I have enjoyed her books and her witty, insightful blog posts.

In 2006, Lee's husband, Bob Woodruff, had a brilliant future ahead of him. The *ABC News* journalist had secured the coveted *World News Tonight* co-anchor chair, after veteran anchor Peter Jennings died. The Woodruffs had planned a family trip to Disney World in January. At the last minute, Bob was sent to Iraq to broadcast on the eve of President George W. Bush's State of the Union address. The family went to Orlando without him.

Embedded with an Iraqi army unit, Bob was struck by a roadside bomb filled with rocks. He sustained a severe head wound that should have killed him. Military medical personnel treated Bob because he was injured on a military mission. As civilians, the Woodruffs found themselves on the perimeter of a close-knit community. They witnessed the bond and kinship that exists within the military, particularly among those who sustain the most horrific injuries.

The Woodruffs faced the prospect that the man who thrived on reporting breaking news had a traumatic brain injury from which he could either die or be permanently impaired. Amazingly, after lying comatose for thirty-six days, Bob recovered. He later returned to work—but not to the anchor chair.

Always one to keep a journal, Lee chronicled her way through Bob's recovery. What began as a therapeutic exercise morphed into a book titled *In an Instant*. Lee, with Bob's contribution, reveals how they dealt with their trauma, while struggling to keep their family intact. The memoir includes lessons learned in the trenches.

In 2010, Lee elaborated on those lessons in a speech at the University of Minnesota, where she entertained doctors and donors with her charm, candor, and insight. Like many who survive tragedy, Lee became reflective about life. She credits their four children with teaching her to slow down, observe the little moments, and laugh at herself; and Bob, with showing her that anything is possible.

Her talk centered on the new lens through which she views life. She became acutely aware of how little time we spend in the present. Our minds scroll ahead to thoughts of work deadlines and dinner plans. The key to life is to take those mere seconds and stretch them; to ignore the dinner dishes and embrace our loved ones when the opportunity arises.

Acknowledging we will all suffer in life, Lee observed, "Sorrow is sorrow, and fear is fear, and loss is loss; and we humans are all traveling on the same bandwidth of life."

Confronted with the daunting task of caring for both Bob and her children, she adopted the mantra, "I am one mommy, and I am doing the best I can."

Lee relied upon a large support network, which included her close friend, Melanie Bloom. Melanie's husband, David Bloom, a journalist and Minnesota native, had died while reporting from Iraq. To Lee, Melanie provided the intuitive support of one who has traveled a similar path, much as my friend Ann and I have done for each other since we lost our husbands.

Bob and Lee dealt with dozens of medical professionals and

discovered that some communicate better than others. Early on, doctors outlined so many potential risks Lee struggled to remain hopeful about Bob's prognosis. One of the greatest things that Bob's nurses did, she said, was share other patients' success stories. Those stories bred hope.

Lee prodded the physicians to be mindful of caregivers and family members when they deliver difficult news. "If you beat the hope out of them at the outset, how can a family be expected to move forward?" To her mind, finding a physician with great hands and a bedside manner is like winning the lottery.

Part of Lee's survival strategy was to wrap herself in a cloak of humor, bordering on irreverence. With a twinkle in her eye, she told the audience, "I am the only wife in Westchester County, New York, who can truly say that her husband has rocks in his head." I loved that comment; far too often, humor has eluded me in my struggles.

When I met Lee, it was chilly outside, drizzling intermittently, and I was feeling a bit blue. As we spoke, the parallels in our lives unfurled—writer and speaker; mother of four (one with special needs); hardworking husband who was frequently away from home; family upended by a horrific event. While I was eager to hear her story, I was mindful that while she nearly lost her husband, I did lose mine. Yet, when we parted, I wished she lived closer, for there is a special bond one shares with another who survives the unimaginable.

Lee's laugh, her clever use of language, and her upbeat view stayed with me. I felt our encounter was serendipitous, for she gave me a precious gift. She reminded me that to get through life's tough stuff one must balance heavy with light—and keep a sense of humor. I've put her words in the pocket in which I house my most cherished lessons about how to navigate life.

The Woodruff family's story is raw and wrenching, but it has an enviable outcome: few who sustain an injury as severe as Bob's recover as he did. With Bob among the lucky survivors, the Woodruffs embraced the healing power of helping others. Recognizing the considerable challenges injured veterans encounter, they established the Bob Woodruff Foundation in 2007. Described as a national organization with a grassroots reach, its mission is to ensure that injured service members thrive after they return stateside. The organization helps injured post 9-11 veterans find programs and resources to help them successfully reintegrate into their communities.

The Woodruffs' work has been praised at the highest level of the military. Admiral Michael Mullen, 17th Chairman of the Joint Chiefs of Staff, said of them, "Their foundation is the gold standard in our country right now . . . a foundation that we know, when we give a dollar, we know it's going to be well spent. And led by Bob and Lee Woodruff—there is no more dedicated couple to our men and women who served than the Woodruffs."

Imperfect Moms

I KNEW WHEN WE MET I had found a kindred spirit in Lee Woodruff. But when I learned her second book was titled *Perfectly Imperfect*, there was no doubt. I'd written a column about being an imperfect mom a few months earlier, in observance of Mother's Day 2009.

. . .

The bags were packed, the boarding passes printed. My passport rested on my desk, unopened since I last used it in 2007. Months of planning this save-my-sanity getaway would soon culminate in an escape from a frigid, gloomy winter. Hours before our scheduled departure, Ted breezed into my office, picked up my passport and stared at it, until he uttered the jaw-dropping words: "Did you realize your passport expired two weeks ago?"

I had spent hours on the Internet reading traveler reviews to ensure I picked just the right spot, and got the very best deal. I had retrieved my passport from the lock box but never thought to actually open it. In my quest to ensure we stayed at a safe and affordable resort with good food and potable water, I overlooked the one detail that was crucial to the trip.

The die cast, we had limited options. Ted could take the two teenage girls who eagerly awaited the trip to Puerto Vallarta and leave me at home to pay my penance. Or we could regroup and make a new plan.

Roughly twelve hours later, the four of us emerged from our plane, tired but transported. Having survived the dreadful winter by dreaming of the lush tropical forest of Puerto Vallarta, I found myself staring at the dusty brown desert of Phoenix, Arizona, with little enthusiasm. For months, I had carried a different picture in my mind.

Formulated in just a few hours, the details of the trip to Phoenix were as slapdash as those of the trip to Puerto Vallarta were meticulous. And yet, we had a great time, mostly because my fellow travelers were determined to make it so. I had little choice but to follow their lead and enjoy the lovely resort I had never heard of before I checked in for the week.

With such a blunder, I couldn't ignore the obvious lesson: despite my perfectionist tendencies, I am, in fact, an imperfect mom. A humbling reminder, but an important one. After all, there is a lot of pressure to be a perfect mom and to have perfect children.

But if I can accept that I am imperfect, that I cannot control everything that happens to my children or me, and choose to make the best of the adversity that is part of life's promise, then I can live life with a peaceful heart—even if I end up in the desert instead of at the ocean.

part
six

*Call
to Action*

Step Forward or Step Back?

THE BOSTON MARATHON has been a tradition for more than one hundred years. Though it is typically an uplifting event, the 2013 marathon was marked by terrorism and tragedy. The incident prompted me to think about mettle, to consider how I would respond in such a crisis. Would I risk my life to save a stranger? When sirens are blaring, would I—and do others—step forward or step back?

On April 22, 1997, I was planted just past the finish line at the 101st Boston Marathon, eyes straining for Ted and our friend John. They were middle-aged guys who had earned coveted spots on the starting line by contributing to Boston's Dana-Farber Cancer Institute. They were the plodding runners whose goal was to finish in as close to four hours as possible.

I spotted them as the weekend warriors took their last steps, clasped hands and danced over the line, before wrapping themselves in the shiny silver space blankets that broadcast, "I made it." That evening we celebrated, all of us with full hearts, and some of us with sore feet.

Marathon runners overcome considerable challenges and obstacles just to get to the starting line. They must discipline themselves to eat and drink the right food and beverages, to get adequate sleep, and take thousands of steps to ready their bodies for the grueling event.

On race day, they focus on weather conditions and jockey for optimal placement at the start. They expect to lose toenails, get cramps, and acquire blisters, but look forward to celebrating their accomplishment after they've crossed the finish line.

Sixteen years after I was a spectator on the streets of Boston, I watched on television as more than 23,000 men and women from around the world laced their shoes and began the prestigious marathon. They ran mile after mile, never anticipating that first responders would greet or treat many of them. They expected to end the day as Ted and John had, with the satisfaction of accomplishing an athletic feat exclusive to few. Instead, those who took more than four hours to finish the race experienced terror, not exhilaration, at the finish line. Two brothers—terrorists—sabotaged the event by planting bombs in backpacks.

In a race that is all about time, thousands were directed away from the finish line, without experiencing the jubilation of crossing it, or learning how long it took them to do so. It's not difficult to imagine the gamut of emotions they felt—fear, anger, sadness, and disappointment. But how does one grouse about not finishing the marathon, if he was lucky enough to escape with his life when hundreds of others lost limbs and lives?

Watching others run marathons always engenders feelings of awe and envy, and a shameful recognition that I will never put one foot in front of another for 26.2 miles, alongside octogenarians, soldiers bearing full combat gear, and mothers pushing strollers. They have a commitment to and a passion for running that I simply lack.

But those of us who don't run marathons can still experience what it feels like to hit the wall and push through it, to achieve something we feared was unattainable. Sometimes we invite challenges—bucket list items such as publishing a first novel, jumping from an airplane, or traveling abroad alone. Other times, challenges arrive unbidden, from an endless list: unemployment, autism, Crohn's disease, bipolar disorder, diabetes, heart disease, bullying, hearing loss, multiple sclerosis, bankruptcy, death, divorce, tornadoes, floods . . . .

Everyone has stuff.

The uninvited challenges provoke uncomfortable questions about who we are and how we react to adversity. Do we face difficult circumstances with grace and courage . . . or surrender to them? Like marathon runners, can we find the fortitude and determination to face the hurdle, even if the best antidotes—resolve, faith, resilience, and support—may be shaky, elusive, or absent?

Aside from our own challenges, how do we respond when others are in need? In Boston, runners, bystanders, and first responders raced toward the impact zone, ignorant of what had caused the explosions, but determined to lend a hand. Residents opened their homes to strangers who needed a place to sleep. They sent pizzas to those who needed sustenance. They offered rides to those who were stranded, and loaned cellphones to those who needed to make vital connections.

When sirens are blaring, do we run toward them or away from them? That is to say, when word comes that an acquaintance has succumbed to cancer, do we attend the wake or find an excuse to skip an uncomfortable tradition? Do we decide against sending a sympathy card because we didn't know the person well? Or do we send a card, assuming any kind words may be welcome to one who is grieving?

If a couple divorces, do we take sides, or let the friendship slip away altogether?

When a friend loses a spouse, do we invite her to join couples for dinner on Saturday night?

In the 2013 marathon, runners from varied backgrounds, cultures, and countries discovered that grief, fear, and crushing disappointment are universal. It is our response to the events that distinguishes and defines us.

I've wrestled with hesitation and ambivalence and learned that, while at times uncomfortable, action rarely engenders regret, but inaction almost always breeds lingering twinges of guilt and remorse. Sometimes we humans just need to dig deep to force ourselves to step forward, not back.

Kevin Warren's Broken Glass

THE YEARS HAVE BROUGHT both blessings and challenges to Kevin Warren. As executive vice president of legal affairs for the Minnesota Vikings, Kevin is the highest-ranking African American executive in both the Vikings organization and the National Football League.

Kevin grew up in Arizona, the youngest of seven children spanning twenty years. Both parents were educators who expected their children to become well-educated, well-mannered, humble, hardworking, and relentless in their pursuits.

He worked hard at both academics and athletics, and leveraged a basketball and pair of sneakers to finance his education. His desire to play college basketball took him first to Penn State then to Arizona State University. Ultimately, he found his place at Grand Canyon University, where he earned his undergraduate business degree. He went on to earn an MBA from Arizona State University, and a law degree from Notre Dame.

Husband to Greta, and father to two bright and athletic teenagers, Kevin has scored big. Yet he is no stranger to adversity. At age twelve, he almost died when a car struck him. He spent six months recuperating in a body cast. More significant, though, was an incident that occurred when he was just ten. The harsh introduction to bigotry prompted a lesson-filled conversation with his grandmother.

"Big Mama," Kevin's petite maternal grandmother, worked as a housekeeper in Paradise Valley, Arizona. One day, Big Mama took

Kevin to work with her. When he asked the homeowner for a glass of water, she handed him what he remembers as a beautiful glass. Kevin drank the water, rinsed out the glass and left it in the kitchen. When he later spotted it in the garbage, he told Big Mama he was afraid he had broken the glass.

The woman with a second grade education assured him he had not broken the glass. Rather, his skin color had prompted her employer to throw it away. That day Big Mama shared six lessons by which Kevin has lived his life.

"Always remember," she counseled, "life is not fair."

"Understand the value of education. Get as much as you can so you are not in a position where someone can throw your glass away."

"Love to work. Don't be lazy."

"Be humble, regardless of your blessings."

"Leave more than you take, in every situation or relationship."

"Make sure you love God."

The soft-spoken man with an imposing physical presence has spent much of his career working in the professional sports world, as an agent for professional athletes, and as legal counsel for the St. Louis Rams, the Detroit Lions, and the Minnesota Vikings. He's thoughtfully charted his professional course, with counsel from both his late father and his wife's father.

As a private attorney in Arizona, Kevin played an instrumental role in the Wilf family's purchase of the Minnesota Vikings franchise. After the deal was consummated, the Warrens moved to Minnesota, for what Kevin assumed would be a brief tenure with the Vikings. Instead, he put down roots.

Kevin has ambitious professional goals. "We have not had a person of color run an NFL club in its more than ninety years," he said. "I want to put together a group to purchase a franchise and to have some ownership interest in it, no matter how small. I want to be the first African American president of an NFL club. And I want to win another Super Bowl, so I can share the experience with my kids."

In February 2015, Kevin was promoted to chief operating officer for the Vikings, taking him one step closer to achieving his goal.

His success has allowed Kevin and Greta to be generous philanthropists at Notre Dame Law School, where they endowed a scholarship; and in Minneapolis, where they support needy school children and families dealing with serious health challenges.

I met Kevin in 2013, shortly after his fiftieth birthday. He was reflective about the past, present, and future.

"This life goes fast," he said. "If I died today, what would my legacy be? It took me forty years to finally recognize the only one I had something to prove to was me. I spent the first half of my life trying to be substantial. I want to spend the next half of my life helping others to be substantial."

Early in life, Kevin found himself at a critical crossroads. When he was injured, he could have easily allowed himself to become bitter. When his grandmother schooled him on bigotry, he could have become bitter. Instead, he worked through his challenges. He has chosen to be better—and to help others to be better, too. His success illustrates the importance of a positive attitude. Moreover, it demonstrates the impact mentors can have in shaping young lives.

You'll Never Amount to Anything

I MET DARRELL THOMPSON at the same networking breakfast where I'd met Kevin Warren a year earlier. As Darrell spoke to the gathering of business professionals, he was a bit self-deprecating; but he had an important message about helping young people to navigate life. Like many of us, he had an embarrassing experience in his formative years that not only had a lasting impact, but also shaped his future. A teacher's tongue-lashing also underscored an important lesson: words are powerful; their impact lingers; *words matter*.

When he was a schoolboy many years ago, Darrell decided to be playful with a substitute teacher. It was an innocuous stunt to which she took offense. He signed the attendance sheet twice. Though his attempt at humor escaped her, it wrought a scathing prediction he never forgot: "You will not amount to anything."

Darrell realized that not everyone would believe in him, so he needed to believe in himself. He graduated from high school in Rochester, Minnesota, then went on to become one of the best players to ever wear a University of Minnesota Golden Gophers uniform. At the end of the 2014 season, the two-time team MVP remained the only Minnesota Gopher to rush for more than 4,000 yards.

Less than one percent of college players advance to the pros. Darrell hadn't planned to play pro football until scouts began courting him. During one meeting, a scout asked him what he wanted to do after football, adding, "Don't tell me you want to work with kids."

That was precisely what he planned to do.

When Darrell signed with the Green Bay Packers in 1990, he was a handful of classes shy of a college diploma—and remains so today. The first-round draft pick played sixty games in five seasons before the Packers cut him.

After he hung up his cleats, he returned to Minneapolis, where he joined Bolder Options, an organization that meshes his passions for mentoring, physical activity, and education. Bolder Options serves youth ages ten to fourteen who are headed for trouble without the right intervention.

The typical Bolder Options participant is a high-risk eleven-year-old boy from a single-parent family. He often may be acting out at school or not attending regularly. Family members may be incarcerated or involved with drugs. These kids are often exposed to violence, drugs, death, divorce, and mental and physical illness at a young age.

Bolder Options matches boys and girls with mentors who can make a one-year commitment of an average of two to four hours per week. The pairs spend time in the community: biking and running and talking about how to manage life's challenges. Through partnerships with schools and other nonprofits, Bolder Options staff and volunteers provide kids a window into the world outside of the one with which they are most familiar. They share an optimistic message about opportunity, while stressing the importance of hard work.

To open young eyes to possibilities that may be invisible to them, speakers talk about professions as disparate as law enforcement and real estate. Staff members underscore the importance of education and healthy habits such as exercise and nutrition. They talk about anger management and sexuality, and tutor middle school students after school.

Darrell, whose parents divorced when he was five, believes

young people need to understand that, while tough things will happen, they don't need to dictate your future. Positive relationships and good decision-making can help kids be whatever they want to be. But to get to that point, they need to be shepherded along the way, just like Darrell.

Brothers for a Lifetime

TORAN MARKS was nine years old when he met Erik Gonring, a Marquette University sophomore. Their lives could not have been more different. Erik grew up with two brothers and both parents in Libertyville, Illinois, a picturesque community located between Chicago and Milwaukee.

Unlike Erik, Toran had no father in his Milwaukee home. His world was small. He didn't have many opportunities to leave the area. He had few male role models. But his mother and grandmother were very present in his life and they expected much from him.

Erik's parents, Matt and Maggie, are so close to me they are more like family than friends. Generous volunteers and mentors, Matt and Maggie are the antithesis of the teacher who shamed Darrell Thompson for a youthful prank. They are active volunteers in their community. Matt is not just an engaged father; he is also a committed mentor for other young men and women, including Dan. So it was natural for their son Erik to step forward and become a mentor.

Had they lived in Minneapolis, Toran and Erik, both athletes, would have been ideal candidates for Bolder Options. Instead, they connected through Big Brothers and Big Sisters in Milwaukee. Through nearly 400 affiliates worldwide, Big Brothers and Big Sisters opens doors for young people who deal with adversity. "Bigs" participate in school or community-based mentoring by spending a few hours with their "littles" a couple times per month. Mentors are trained; matches are made carefully.

Matt and Maggie set a high bar for their boys. Erik set the same bar for Toran. He encouraged his little brother to work hard in school and to set his sights on college. Their mutual interest in sports offered a natural pathway into their relationship. Over the years, Erik and Toran have spent many hours together at sporting events.

As their relationship—and Toran—matured, Erik shared wise counsel from one of his own mentors. Years ago, as they sat in a hot tub looking at Lake Michigan in the distance, Erik's Uncle Mike told his sons and nephews that their lives were full of possibility as long as they avoided four buoys. Any of the buoys—an unwanted pregnancy, a felony conviction, addiction, or debt—could alter the direction of their lives forever.

While the buoys were within their control, cancer was not. In 2009, Erik, an elite triathlete, was diagnosed with Hodgkin's lymphoma. During his treatment, he didn't get to spend much time with his little brother. Yet while Erik was fighting for his life, Toran was focused on improving his own. He earned the highest GPA in his eighth grade class and became the valedictorian.

Despite his illness, Erik was not going to miss his little brother's graduation, or his speech. He traveled to Milwaukee for Toran's graduation and listened with pride as the middle school graduate talked about how Erik had set a high bar and challenged him to reach it.

Their relationship didn't go unnoticed. Their Big Brothers Big Sisters chapter selected them as Male Match of the Year. The chapter planned to recognize them at the fall banquet. But Erik had a frightening development that precluded him from making the trip. His chemotherapy had failed to eradicate his cancer. The twenty-five-year-old elite triathlete had to undergo a stem cell transplant. Instead of appearing at the banquet in person, he made a video with Toran that was shown at the event.

Fortunately, the transplant was successful, and Erik reclaimed his health and his life. Living and working in Chicago, he sent Toran a train ticket to the windy city to expand the young man's horizons beyond Milwaukee.

He also invited him to his uncle's cottage in Michigan. While Erik had grown up spending time at the lake, Toran had never been to a lake home. His weekend with Erik, and a dozen of his relatives, was an eyeopener for all.

As they've gone through life's transitions, Erik and Toran, both adults now, have remained active in each other's lives. Erik helped Toran evaluate his college options. When Toran chose Grinnell College, Erik helped him to apply for scholarships and financial aid. When Erik was married in 2014, Toran served as an usher.

While some pairs don't last, Erik never imagined that their relationship would end. Their special bond is about more than being a big or little brother. Erik believes the real value of mentoring occurs over the course of a lifetime.

"You are setting yourself up for a friendship. You are getting involved in a meaningful relationship that you should have for the rest of your life."

Mary Jo Copeland's Great Love

MARY JO COPELAND is a small woman with a big footprint in Minnesota. While her work earned her the prestigious Presidential Citizens Medal, relatively few know about her early life. The soft-spoken woman barely graduated from high school and never attended college. Yet since 1985, the director of Minneapolis' Sharing and Caring Hands has raised millions of dollars to provide a safety net to needy people—without government or United Way funds.

Author Michelle Hinck and Mary Jo met when Michelle volunteered at the nonprofit. Watching Mary Jo wash the feet of strangers who needed a shower and clean clothes, she sensed that someone with such passion and purpose must have quite a story. Michelle spent hours shadowing Mary Jo and meeting with her husband, Dick, to gather material for *Great Love: The Mary Jo Copeland Story*. First published in 2003, the revised biography was released in 2012.

Great Love recounts a life filled with neglect, fear, compassion, and giving. Mary Jo was born in 1942, shortly before her father left for the war. Her father's parents persuaded his wife to move into their Minneapolis home, though they viewed her as a second-class, unworthy farm girl. But their granddaughter was a different story. Her grandmother and aunts doted on Mary Jo, doing their best to ensure she formed no emotional attachment to her mother.

Mary Jo's father returned from the war with an injury and an explosive temper. He moved his wife and daughter into a home of their own. Mary Jo watched her father beat her mother daily. He subjected his young daughter to frequent verbal tirades and occasional physical assaults that still haunt her.

With the arrival of a baby boy, Mary Jo's weary mother neglected her daughter's basic needs. Mary Jo often wore dirty clothes and bathed in a filthy bathtub. Her mother once packed garbage in her lunch bag.

Terrified of her father, Mary Jo found solace in church and prayer. She yearned to do the will of God and planned to become a nun. However, at age fifteen, she met and fell for Dick Copeland at a high school dance. Despite family objections, they married after high school. Estranged from both families, Mary Jo and Dick had twelve children in quick succession.

Mary Jo ran her household on a schedule that began at 5:00 a.m. and ended after dark. Though the children had chores, her time was consumed by providing the clean home and clothes, and the good meals she missed in her own childhood. As Dick worked long hours, Mary Jo became reclusive, depressed, and dependent on Valium. Seeking guidance through prayer, she weaned herself off the Valium and ventured outside the home when the children were in school.

She became a volunteer at Catholic Charities in Minneapolis. Over the course of three years she found the experience gratifying, frustrating, and educational. She discovered she has no patience for rules and institutional bureaucracy, which she viewed as a hindrance to doing God's work. She had her own ideas about how to most effectively serve the people in need. Though her intentions were good, the charity didn't welcome her methods and ideas.

After parting ways with Catholic Charities, she started the organization that runs by her rules. A self-described "loose cannon," she acknowledges that not everyone likes what she does, particularly city officials with whom she has battled. Nevertheless, with limited paid staff and hundreds of volunteers, Mary Jo has raised more than $100 million in the past thirty years.

Her early years instilled the empathy that makes Mary Jo's work so extraordinary. She understands the indignity of filth; the challenge of addiction; and the terror of abuse. "Getting out of your own pain and into someone else's doesn't take it away, but it gives you peace. Instead of concentrating on the pain and hard times and suffering in your own life, you are concentrating on someone else to help them."

God called her to her work, she says. "With the gifts that I had, I think it would have been a horrible disappointment had I not done what I was called to do. When people don't listen to what they need to do, they get depressed. Had I not listened, I probably would have been a very depressed woman."

Though she lives with a lot of suffering and memories, she greets every day with gratitude. "I get up grateful that I can make a difference in the life of someone else; that I can feel what they feel. It's a gift from God and a privilege that is mine."

Mary Jo Copeland's commitment to helping the needy was contagious. A few months after I met her, Jack and I went Christmas shopping. We picked out books, tablets, crayons, socks, and hats. We took them to Sharing and Caring Hands, hoping we would brighten the holiday for families we'd never meet. It was gratifying to share the experience with my son, who loves children, and to open his eyes to a world in which others do not have the comforts we take for granted.

The Fraser Legacy

LIKE MARY JO COPELAND, Louise Fraser endured weighty personal challenges. Yet both women dedicated their lives to helping others. Had they chosen to step forward because of (or despite) their own difficulties?

In her lifetime, Louise suffered great loss but bestowed great gifts. Born in 1894 and orphaned by age three, the free-spirited and strong-willed girl was raised by a prim and proper aunt whose strict discipline often frustrated her.

Early on, Louise had an affinity for children who struggled. As a young teacher, she was often assigned the problem children. Her school principal once counseled her to give a difficult student a good spanking so he would behave. Her instincts told her the boy just needed a little love.

Beginning in 1920, Louise experienced a series of tragedies. Her three-year-old son fell from a moving car and died. Her husband, a federal agent, was shot to death while investigating a moonshine operation. Her eldest daughter died from a staph infection while attending law school. But her younger daughter Jean's challenges set the course for Louise's exceptional life.

Jean contracted spinal meningitis when she was six weeks old. Though she recovered, she behaved wildly and was considered "retarded" until age eleven, when doctors discovered she was stone deaf. She could hear very high sounds and very low sounds—but not the sounds typical of conversation.

While they awaited an opening in a school for the deaf, Louise discovered that if she played music she could expand Jean's attention span and teach her some of the skills she lacked. In the 1930s, it was hardly the norm to teach children with special needs at home. The "feeble minded" were typically institutionalized. They were medicated, segregated, and not educated.

As word spread of Louise's approach with Jean, reactions were mixed. Some parents persuaded Louise to teach their "retarded" children. Some professionals objected to her methodology.

The opposition didn't deter Louise. By 1941 she was schooling twenty-five students in her home. Problems plagued her. When neighbors complained to local officials, she was forced to relocate in a commercial building that soon proved inadequate. The widow, who earned a pittance, raised money with other parents and mortgaged her home so she could move to a more suitable location.

In the 1950s, Louise was able to hire the school's first full-time music teacher. Critics eventually became allies. One of her early skeptics—a university physician who labeled her a fraud—praised her excellent work and acknowledged the need for educational services for exceptional children. By the early 1960s, the school was serving sixty children ages three to twenty and gaining national recognition.

In 2013, Fraser served 9,300 clients with myriad mental health and developmental disorders, seventy percent with autism. Over the years, Fraser expanded its service to include diagnosis, multi-disciplinary treatment, and support services for children, adolescents, adults, and their families. Fraser has added transition services for youth, and expanded the residential program that serves my own son. Unlike years past, neighbors have commended Fraser residents for being "great neighbors."

The work of the woman who lived in abject poverty to ensure Fraser remained viable endures, as do words that offer insight into her soul. Not long before her death in 1981, Louise wrote the following in a book entitled, *A Cup of Kindness: A Book for Parents of Retarded Children.*

> *Did you ever feel the confidence of a little child's hand in yours? It is silent communication that expresses security and trust. It is a silent asking of guidance through the entanglement of confusion in untraveled ways. You give these things to the child when you give your hand to him. You are the privileged one. Yours is true service, for it must come from the heart if it is to fulfill that earnest appeal felt in the little outstretched hand of a child in need of security.*

Consistent leadership and growth have marked Fraser. For the past twenty-five years, Diane Cross has been at the helm. In 1989, Diane was a speech audiologist and director of medical rehabilitation and education at Courage Center, a Minneapolis rehabilitation facility for people with disabilities. She had a newborn and a two-year-old, and wanted to spend more time with them than the Courage Center job afforded.

Believing it would be less stressful than her Courage Center job, Diane accepted the offer to become Fraser's CEO. She couldn't have been more wrong. During her first week on the job, she discovered the carpet was held together by duct tape, the ceilings leaked, and the organization could not make payroll. It was at a tipping point.

To stop the financial hemorrhaging, Diane fired the janitor and garbage pickup service. She and staff took turns cleaning the building. She froze salaries and renegotiated contracts. Rather than spending more time with her family, Diane slept at her office during her first week on the job.

With the reality of her decision becoming increasingly obvious, Diane decided she was led to the position for a reason: it was her job to salvage Fraser. She resolved that Fraser was not going to fail on her watch. When she became demoralized, she recalled Louise Fraser's struggles and success.

●

Within a year, with the help of a dedicated staff and board of directors, Diane had taken the organization's balance sheet from red to black. But Fraser needed outside help in order to survive. Diane took it all on: fundraising, accounting, human resources, and marketing. She shored up the board of directors, designed a vision, and rallied others to support it. The organization not only survived, it flourished.

Diane's sons are grown now, and their mother is a well-respected CEO and advocate for her constituents. The feisty redhead has demonstrated her tenacity, relentless work ethic, and loyalty. With a forty-million-dollar annual budget and one thousand employees, Fraser has ambitious plans for a growing number of people, always focused on its mantra: special needs, bright futures.

Coach Jerry Kill: Chasing Dreams

WHEN JERRY KILL accepted the head coach position at the University of Minnesota in late 2010, his sights were on transforming a struggling football program. But his wife Rebecca sensed the move would be about more than football.

Off the field, Jerry and Rebecca had been dealing with the coach's health issues for years. When a seizure landed him in the hospital in 2005, doctors discovered he had undiagnosed stage-four kidney cancer. The seizure may have been a lifesaver; without it they may not have discovered the cancer in time.

By the time they moved to Minnesota, the cancer was gone but the epilepsy persisted. When "Coach" was on the sidelines during his first season, he shocked players and viewers by experiencing a seizure in a home game against New Mexico State. The stadium was hushed as medical personnel tended to Coach and transported him off the field on a gurney.

The assistant coaches who had been with Jerry for years were familiar with the seizures that began in 2000. Defensive coordinator Tracy Claeys took on the head coach duties for the rest of the New Mexico State game. For the remainder of the season, Jerry coached from the press box while Tracy, his longtime assistant, managed the game from the sidelines.

Vicki Kopplin, executive director of Epilepsy Foundation of Minnesota, had longed for a high-profile individual to partner with her organization. An estimated three million Americans live with epilepsy, though many are private about it, fearful that if they disclose it they will lose their jobs or not be hired at all.

After the sideline incident, Vicki reached out to the coach. Initially, he agreed to help raise awareness, but explained that he and Rebecca were committed to financially supporting their cancer fund they'd started in Illinois after his cancer battle.

In April 2012, the Kills attended the Epilepsy Foundation gala. The evening was a game changer. For the first time, the coach spoke publicly about his condition, using the term epilepsy instead of seizure disorder. Epilepsy carried negative connotations—and sounded too scary. But, in a room full of adults and children who shared his condition, Coach realized others were struggling far more than he, plagued by false stereotypes and stigma. In an unscripted speech, he spoke candidly about his experience to a receptive crowd.

Though there are more than twenty different types of seizures, people most often think of tonic clonic (grand mal) seizures when they hear about epilepsy. The person who experiences a seizure can lose consciousness and control, experience jerking motions, muscle stiffening, and falls. Seizures can be more frightening to observers than to the person who experiences them. But they are disorienting. After regaining consciousness, Coach has often asked whether he hurt anyone while seizing.

Absence seizures are harder to identify. A person who is staring off into space may appear to be suffering from attention deficit disorder or just daydreaming, when he is actually having a seizure. In the coach's case, he will have a cluster of seizures then go through a dormant period. Rebecca has been at her husband's side during every seizure and thought they were not as scary as they looked. However, years after her husband's seizures began, Rebecca learned they could be fatal.

Parents field many difficult questions from children, foremost among them, "Am I going to die from this?" Wayne Drash is a writer for CNN and the father of a ten-year-old son who began having seizures at age seven. Wayne has held his son Billy during seizures and answered his questions, such as why they happen and whether they can be fatal. Wayne says every one of the more than 500 times his son has seized up—in the school lunchroom, at the top of the stairs in their home, in the swimming pool—he has lost a bit of his own soul.

People drown and suffocate from seizures, so Billy has given up favorite activities such as swimming and biking. The family has exhausted efforts to control the seizures, at enormous expense. They've tried medications and investigated medical marijuana, even considering a move to Colorado, where it is legal.

But Coach Kill is an inspiration to the young boy who is often physically bruised from falling and emotionally drained from teasing at school. When Billy has a seizure, his dad reminds him that he is just like the coach he saw interviewed for a CNN segment.

Though Coach may help kids like Billy to accept and manage a condition that strikes with no warning, it was the children who inspired Jerry and Rebecca to start the Chasing Dreams fund in 2014. They made a substantial donation of their own, and are using their platform to help raise more for a summer camp for kids with epilepsy. The money will also support an educational program for students, parents, and professionals.

Both adults and children use words like "freak" to describe a condition that arrives with no warning and leaves the person fearful, angry, confused, and depleted. After Jerry's first sideline seizure, a Minneapolis sports columnist described the coach as "the subject of pity and ridicule" and called for his resignation. But family and supporters fought back, and the columnist recanted his position.

Rebecca insists that epilepsy does not define a person. Of the man she married at age nineteen, she says, "If I took all the minutes when Jerry's had seizures, they wouldn't even add up to one day out of the fifty-three years of his life."

Jerry has made dramatic changes in his attitude and approach toward his epilepsy. He understands his condition requires on-going monitoring and tweaking. He is more vigilant about his diet, exercise, sleep, and stress management. With a new physician and Rebecca closely monitoring his lifestyle, he limits soda and coffee, and sleeps more than a couple of hours per night.

The couple that began their marriage living in a trailer now earns a handsome income. Jerry, the first in his family to graduate from college, is optimistic that brilliant minds will eventually figure out epilepsy, so children like Billy aren't bullied on the playground.

Jerry Kill is living his dream with the woman he fell in love with, at first sight. As he continues to develop the Golden Gophers football program, Coach advises others to ignore the naysayers. He encourages them to do whatever they can to make *their* own dreams come true.

The Blood of 200 Heroes

I HAD NEVER CONSIDERED being a blood or marrow donor, until Julia became ill. When she needed a bone marrow donor to survive her illness, I realized how critical it is for people to submit to an uncomfortable procedure that yields an immeasurable payoff.

I'd also never been a blood donor. Willingly get poked by needles? I think not.

Then I took Julia to the outpatient clinic at the University of Minnesota, where she received pint after pint of blood cells from anonymous benefactors we never met. How could we repay the debt? I stepped forward and became a regular blood donor. The needle prick no longer concerns me. I'm gratified by the thought that I might help to save another's life, as many did for my daughter.

Julia wasn't the only little girl to be saved by strangers. On Valentine's Day 2011, I shared a story in the *Pioneer Press* about another child who was saved by donors.

. . .

This Valentine's Day, many will celebrate with gifts of jewelry, chocolate, or by sharing a meal at a favorite restaurant. Angie MacDonald and her family will mark the day with gratitude for more than 200 strangers who saved her life thirty-one Valentine's Days ago.

Born prematurely to Charles and Cece MacDonald of West St. Paul in 1970, Angie spent much of the first decade of her life in hospitals. As a newborn, she developed an infection when a catheter was inserted in her umbilical vein. Complications ensued, and she developed varicose veins in her esophagus and stomach.

Every few months Angie was hospitalized with internal bleeding. She typically received one or two units of blood, was stabilized, and released. Her child-sized veins were not substantial enough to tolerate the surgery that would correct the problem. The goal was to get her to age ten, when the surgical repair was expected to be more successful. She almost made it.

On February 12, 1980, nine-and-a-half-year-old Angie was rushed to St. Paul Children's Hospital with massive bleeding. The blood flowed in fits and starts but could not be stopped. Once again, things got complicated. A needle punctured her lung, causing it to collapse. She went into cardiac arrest. On Valentine's Day, she was rushed into surgery to sew up the bleeding veins in her esophagus.

Waiting with little paper Valentine's hearts and prayers, her parents were assured there was plenty of blood available to deal with the hemorrhaging. However, as medical personnel worked on her for the next fifteen hours, the two units at the hospital and the additional supply at the local Red Cross facility proved to be inadequate to deal with what Angie refers to as "the big bleed."

Denny Hagglund was responsible for distributing blood for the American Red Cross. He took the call for more blood for Angie. As medical professionals worked their magic in the operating room, Denny worked the phones. Many people owed him favors, so he called them in, sharing Angie's story. The response was amazing.

When he exhausted the blood supply in the Twin Cities, he called other communities around the state. Then he moved on to Nebraska and Wisconsin. They were racing the clock. With many working behind the scenes, nearly 250 units of blood, platelets, and plasma made their way to St. Paul within twenty-four hours.

The call to action dramatically altered Denny's perspective of his job. He worked sixteen hours that first day. At midnight, he was sitting in front of the cooler putting away blood, wondering how the little girl would possibly survive. If she didn't make it, he hoped she would go peacefully. Then he thought about his own daughters, three months and three years old, respectively. Denny had worked for the Red Cross for fifteen years, but until that moment he hadn't thought about the fact that every recipient of the blood products he collected was someone's relative. He told himself he was not going to let the little girl die.

"I kind of adopted little Angie that night."

Over the ensuing months, Angie had more surgeries and more transfusions. Denny asked about Angie every time he called Children's Hospital. A few months later, Angie stopped by the Red Cross with fresh-baked cookies and profound thanks. Denny recalls that there were a couple hundred people in the building in tears that day because they realized a miracle had happened.

As a donor representative for the Red Cross, Denny frequently shares Angie's story when he is trying to solicit donors. When people assert needle phobia as an excuse not to donate, he reminds them that the donation only involves a little pinch and an hour of their time. And he tells them about Angie. He personalizes the need, asking people if they would donate to their sister or daughter; reminding them that every day someone's mother or sister needs blood to live.

Angie's mother Cece has lived every day with gratitude for the strangers who had already donated blood so that when the call went out for more, there was an adequate supply to save Angie's life. It was an act with no direct benefit, but with a profound impact.

Angie is also mindful of the generosity of strangers who stepped forward decades ago.

"I have the blood of 200 heroes in me."

A Little Marrow, a Lot of Life

IN 2005, Julie and Brandon Williams were high school sweethearts who imagined they would have the "perfect little family" in the small town of Milaca, an hour from the Twin Cities. Julie is a special education program supervisor, and Brandon a bus mechanic for the St. Francis School District. Life seemed to be on track when Julie gave birth to their son Luke that summer. Luke was a happy, personable, and healthy baby until he developed a respiratory illness that landed him in Children's Hospital of Minneapolis in February 2006.

But Luke was dealing with more than a respiratory virus. Three weeks after his admission, he was diagnosed with myelodysplastic syndrome (MDS), a rare disease in which the bone marrow produces insufficient healthy blood cells. Coincidentally, it was one of the diseases physicians had tested for but ruled out when my daughter Julia was going through a similar experience a year earlier. Like Julia, Luke needed a bone marrow transplant to survive.

With no familial match, the Williams turned to the Minneapolis-based National Marrow Donor Program. The organization matches patients like Luke, with unrelated donors whose HLA tissue type is as close a match to that of the patient as possible. Blood-forming cells can be taken from a donor's umbilical cord blood, or collected from either bone marrow or peripheral blood cells, then introduced into the patient's bloodstream.

It was a few weeks before the Williams family received welcome news. A mother had donated umbilical cord blood that could be used to treat Luke's disease. In early April 2006, Luke was admitted to the new children's hospital at the University of Minnesota for his transplant. Five months later, the family returned to Milaca to commence their "new normal."

Three years after Luke's diagnosis, Julie delivered a baby girl they named Molly. At Molly's two-year checkup, Julie asked to have her toddler's blood checked. It wasn't standard to do so, but her mother's intuition told her something was amiss.

A few weeks passed before Julie and Brandon received unfathomable news: Molly had the same rare disease from which Luke had been cured.

Since her big brother couldn't be her donor, the family turned to the National Marrow Donor Program once again. Another guardian angel came to their rescue. Exactly five years after Luke was born, the Williams returned to the children's hospital and went through the grueling process all over again with Molly, using umbilical cord blood from a different donor. Like her big brother, Molly was cured of MDS. But each year they return to the university for follow-up testing, always watchful for long-term effects or complications.

Most unrelated donors are between eighteen and forty-four years old because their cells lead to more successful transplants. Laura Gintant joined the registry at age twenty-four to honor a friend who succumbed to cancer. A few months later she was surprised to receive a phone call informing her she was a match for a three-year-old cancer patient named Owen. Laura, who lived in suburban Minneapolis, had never undergone surgery. Despite her reservations, she went to the hospital and had her marrow extracted with a large needle. She was home by nightfall.

Owen and Laura met after his transplant. They've stayed

connected. Each year they participate in a fundraising walk together. Laura has encouraged many in her network to join the registry, too. Laura gave Owen another chance at life. She gave his family hope. It's a simple equation for her. Donating bone marrow is a relatively small inconvenience that provides an immeasurable return.

Fill a Stocking

IN OCTOBER 2012, Superstorm Sandy devastated a number of communities on the eastern shore, particularly in New Jersey. Many sent money and prayers. But a Wisconsin woman did much more. Jeanne Murphy Curtis demonstrated that grit, determination, and the willingness to devote one's time could also yield a powerful impact.

More than a month after Superstorm Sandy struck, displaced residents remained hunkered down with friends and relatives, sharing close quarters without familiar comforts of home. Many spent frigid days without coats, and nights without blankets. They had difficulty getting around, as cars had been destroyed and public transportation interrupted.

As I pulled on my winter boots in Minnesota, I couldn't fathom that people in New York or New Jersey lost both socks and boots in swirling seawater. A month earlier, thousands had both homes and mortgages; after the storm, many were left with just the latter.

Jeanne, a Philadelphia native, heard from friends and family in the affected area that babies were left without diapers and women without feminine products. The Wisconsin resident could not abide the notion that she was living in the land of plenty, and not helping people who had nothing. Joining forces with her friends, Kristen and Kimberly, she launched "Call to action! Sandy Hurricane Relief." Though they hoped to secure goods from local corporations, they encountered red tape and responses, such as, "We've already made our donations." Early thoughts of sending boxes of goods gave way when they discovered the high cost of shipping.

They solicited help from KARE11 TV in Minneapolis. The NBC affiliate not only offered its parking lot, it secured a fifty-three-foot truck from a local company. A mutual friend connected Jeanne with a New York priest who acted as a broker, assembling and distributing goods that ultimately arrived from Orthodox Jewish women, Mormons, Methodists, and Catholics.

As Christmas approached, concern shifted to the children who had no home and would have no Christmas. A new initiative—Fill a Stocking—encouraged families like mine to make or purchase stockings, and fill them with socks and mittens, small toys, playing cards, hair ribbons, and more. Those who wanted to contribute could send cookies to families who didn't have a workable oven, or send snowflake cutouts to post on windows, which they did have.

Playing Santa Claus, Father Cunningham distributed presents to children who had lost so much they were excited to receive something as small as a new toothbrush. For both benefactors and recipients, the initiative reinforced the true meaning of Christmas.

Grab Life by the Horns

MAJOR CHARLES CREECH served our country with great pride and distinction, earning two Meritorious Service Medals for outstanding performance and four Air Medals for combat flights. He served in operations Iraqi Freedom and Enduring Freedom. At MacDill Air Force Base, Florida, he was responsible for supporting seven combatant commanders.

In 2010 Chuck was diagnosed with colon cancer. Despite a valiant effort, supported by his wife Sara, a veteran and nurse, he lost the battle in May 2011. He was thirty-seven years old.

I knew Chuck had mounted an intense fight for his life. He and Sara were close friends and neighbors of my sister Traci. When my kids and I went to Tampa for our first Thanksgiving without Ted, Sara and Chuck invited us to stay at their home. They were at MD Anderson Cancer Center in Texas, hoping for a "Hail Mary" treatment.

When I saw Chuck's flight suits hanging in the bedroom where I slept, I was overcome with sadness. Despite his tenacious fight, I suspected the handsome young husband and father would never wear them again.

With a heavy heart in May 2011, I silently welcomed Sara into the freakin' widows club. Sara had served as a surgical nurse in the Air Force. When she returned from her tour in Iraq, she experienced debilitating depression and anxiety. She could no longer work as a nurse. Yet, when Traci shared Sara's eulogy with me, I discovered she was one tough lady.

·

Chuck had many loves in his life: the military and flying fueled his passion for the last decade and a half. He didn't work for the military; he lived and breathed it! A few months ago, we were talking and he reminded me that EVERY time he puts on his uniform, he knows that there is a chance he will be trading his life for his country. Many times the enemies are plentiful, and the dangers are obvious. Sometimes, though, we are forced to confront the unknown and unexpected consequences. Chuck faced both with the same determination and force as any military conflict he served in. This time though, the fight wasn't for his country. No, this time it was for his family, for his children, for his wife. What kept him fighting over the last few difficult months was the desire to protect and care for his family. He wanted them to know . . . to truly grasp the idea that he would give his life for any one of them . . . .

Chuck was never interested in the accolades. I think they even embarrassed him. Whenever someone tried to honor him, he would turn it into something special for those around him. So here it is . . . the lesson he wanted us to learn from him.

None of us will have a perfect life. There will always be conflict, always be tragedy, always disappointment and sadness. But there will also be incredible moments that make this life worthwhile. For Chuck, that meant realizing his dream of attending the Air Force Academy, being able to fly and get paid for it, holding each child for the first time, marrying his true love, buying his first boat, catching the big fish . . . Chuck's motto for fishing was the same for his life: ". . . just five more minutes." What we need to do is to find love and hold onto it with all our might. Find those things that drive your passion and give your life purpose . . . No excuses.

Grab life by the horns, and ride the crap out of it.

Sara took Chuck's words to heart. Later that year she left Florida for Indiana, where she has family. It was time for a new career. She purchased a foreclosed farmhouse located on forty-three acres. Blue Yonder Organic Farm is a labor of love and dedication to the military.

With help from family and veterans programs, as well as her own savings, Sara has made a new life for herself. She began by planting fruit trees, berry bushes, and vegetables. She raises chickens and sells their eggs at the local farmer's market, along with meat and produce. She shares the acreage with lambs and livestock guard dogs.

Blue Yonder was the first veteran farm in Indiana to be certified by the Farmer Veteran Coalition. When she sells her wares at the local farmer's market, Sara proudly displays a "Homegrown by Heroes" sign. Having found healing in farming, Sara is committed to helping other veterans to do the same. She attended an agriculture-training program for veterans. She is developing a training program for veterans who want to get involved in small-scale sustainable farming. She invites veterans groups to visit Blue Yonder to experience life on a farm.

When the Indianapolis National Guard was deployed to Afghanistan, she provided fresh food from the farm to their families. The people in Sara's new community are happy to support a veteran. Buying the food she grows is a way to express thanks for her military service.

In a February 2015 news feature, the young widow described how the new venture has helped her to heal. "I am getting out of bed every day. I am doing my chores every day. I am taking care of animals every day. People are relying on me. I don't know where my life is going to take me, but I feel like I'm on the right path."

part
seven

Moving On

Chuck Dammit

THOUGH IT WAS JULIA'S IDEA to get a dog, we all became attached to Sara, our Cavalier King Charles spaniel. Over the years, we took turns being Sara's favorite. As Julia recovered from her bone marrow transplant and sought normalcy in friends and sports, Sara became my buddy, following me from computer to coffeepot to washing machine.

Sara had an insatiable need for attention and affection. She also had ways of getting her own way, imploring me with her eyes to take her along in the car, or barking until I sheepishly pulled her onto my lap at the dinner table. When I entered our home, she snapped to attention from her perch in the sunroom, tail slapping against the pink leather chair she claimed as her own.

Yet at night, she nestled at Ted's feet as he reclined on the chaise lounge to watch sports, cellphone in one hand and remote control in the other. She hounded Ted for treats, knowing he was an easy mark. Sara was one of Daddy's girls, and Ted adored his girls.

In the weeks after Ted's fatal heart attack, life changed—and so did Sara. At first, a stream of visitors invaded her space. Then commotion gave way to inactivity as we established a new and unsettling normal, punctuated by her labored breathing. When she was diagnosed with congestive heart failure, I wondered whether she, too, had a broken heart.

On a Saturday in April, it was time to say good-bye to Sara. The parting was more painful than I would have imagined. Julia was so devastated she could not bear to go to the animal hospital with us. My dog-loving friend Deb drove me, with Sara wrapped in my arms.

With Sara and Ted gone, Jack living in New Hampshire, and Caitie and Dan living close to each other in Denver, Julia and I adjusted to our new normal, with little discussion about it. Family meals typically involved just the two of us, although most nights a favorite TV show played on the big screen above the fireplace. The meals I prepared were created more out of recognition that a teenage athlete needs nourishment than my own interest in eating them.

In contrast, Julia's concoctions reflected her passion for good food, and were, perhaps, an effort to perpetuate her dad's proclivity for whipping up spontaneous feasts, with her at his side. Most days, housekeeping was simple, in contrast to the days when there were six humans and a canine sharing the same space, and handfuls of soft white fur collecting on the sofa.

We slowly—and reluctantly—became accustomed to the reality that when the doorbell rang, it just rang. The chime was no longer followed by a piercing bark and the scrambling of paws on the hardwood floor as our twenty-pound watchdog raced to greet newcomers, tail wagging frenetically.

As summer ended and fall beckoned, heartfelt words penetrated the silence; my reticent teenager told me the ongoing quiet was unbearable. When her friend acquired a puppy named Cooper, the girls crafted a get Julia-a-canine campaign, subtler than the grade school effort that netted Sara, but steady and persuasive nonetheless. I received text messages with photos of Cooper, and heard tales of how sweet and easy he was to have around. I was counseled on how a dog could offer me comfort, companionship, and security.

Nearly nine years after I capitulated and bought Sara, I found myself on the horns of a dilemma, with the daughter who had lost so much and asked for so little. If she were working me for another pair of boots or a tattoo, I would not have been conflicted. But her request was simple and complicated, uninformed and well reasoned.

She craved commotion and the fullness that a puppy would add to a home that no longer bore any resemblance to the one in which she'd spent her entire life. She wanted to restore energy and life to a formerly hectic household that was utterly lacking in it.

Julia was bound for college and had no intention of taking me with her. Focused on her own life, she couldn't appreciate my reluctance to assume a time-consuming commitment that would continue long after she had left home. Her days with a dog would be numbered; mine long lasting. I'd come to relish spontaneity, with no worry about who would let the dog out.

As I contemplated life as a single empty nester, a young dog felt like a burden that would ultimately rest only in my lap. On the other hand, the pitter-patter of paws on the floor and a reason to go outside during the dreaded winter months had appeal. But the fact that my daughter could bare her soul about how she wanted—needed—to fill the void was the most compelling argument of all.

It wasn't long before Julia and I went to investigate the litter of English cream golden retrievers. We chose the runt, and Julia insisted upon naming him. I was not surprised by her choice of names, as I'd heard them often enough from her dad. "If we get another dog I want to name it Chuck . . . or Dammit." He would demonstrate the appeal of the names: "Come 'ere Dammit. Up Chuck . . ." We weren't going to name our dog Dammit, but I agreed that could be his middle name.

Julia went to the pet store to make his nametag. She called with an unexpected question, later explaining that the adults behind her at the kiosk threw curious glances her way as they overheard our conversation.

"How do I spell Chuck's middle name? Damnit or Dammit?"

As adorable as he was, I remained ambivalent towards Chuck. The last thing I needed in the year from hell was one more responsibility or expense: a potty schedule, a new pooper scooper, vet visits, vaccinations, and more.

Dog-loving friends looked at me with knowing eyes and said, "Just wait. You're going to love him." To my surprise, in the throes of a frigid winter, my heart began to melt. The four-legged guy would bat his deep brown eyes at me, and I'd coo at him, "You are so dang cute."

I watched him chase his littermate and best bud, Cooper, and a belly laugh would begin to percolate within me. As Chuck came to understand that teeth are for balls and bones (not laptop chargers and soccer cleats) I began to come around.

I knew I'd evolved when, one chilly Friday night, he leaped onto my lap as I was stretched out on the chaise lounge, remote control in one hand, glass of wine in the other, and I didn't respond with the usual "Four on the floor, Chuck, four on the floor." Though I rationalized that it was a little cozier with him nestled close by, I couldn't ignore the obvious: I was sheepishly smitten.

Cows Need Love, Too

IN THE FALL OF 2011, Julia began applying for colleges. It was time for her to spread her wings. Though she considered colleges in Minnesota, Iowa, Chicago, and Denver, she settled on the University of Wisconsin-Madison. She'd always been a Badger at heart. When she was a little girl, she once asked me earnestly, "Mom, are you sure I wasn't born in Wisconsin?"

Though I'd tried to engage her in conversation, she rarely spoke to me about her dad. But much like Dan's eulogy at Ted's funeral, Julia's college essay revealed not only her deep love for her dad, but also what she'd learned from him in the fifteen years they spent together. It was another reminder of how, as parents, we are continuously defining our legacy, often without realizing we are doing so.

My dad, Ted Edwin Sullivan, or as we liked to call him, Tedwin, was undoubtedly the best dad on earth, and one of the greatest people I knew. He was kind, funny, smart, caring, and loved his children more than anything. On December 15, 2009, my dad died of a heart attack. It is ironic that a man with such a big heart died because of it. Although he was taken from me much too early, he taught me lessons I will never forget.

Ted lesson number one: "Cows need love, too." When I was in first grade, my dad took me out of school to go fishing in Wisconsin. As we were driving through the farmland, I com-

plained about the smell of cow manure. My dad simply said, "Oh, Julia, cows need love, too!" rolled down his window, and began mooing.

I then rolled down my window and mooed to the cows, too. This statement perfectly fit with my dad's personality—he was that loud guy on the airplane making friends with everyone. He always taught me to be inclusive, even if I did not necessarily like the person. I learned everyone needs a little love, even gross, smelly cows.

Ted lesson number two: Always stop at a lemonade stand. Always. No matter how busy he was, or even if he had already stopped at one, my dad always stopped at a kid's lemonade stand. He considered it supporting the local business. This is a tradition I follow: At the beginning of last summer I got a ten-dollar roll of quarters. I ran out by July.

However, in a larger sense, my dad really taught me to live in the moment and enjoy life. Who cares if you're stressed out on your way to run a million errands? Stop and enjoy a glass of lemonade.

Ted lesson number three: "Don't be a victim." This lesson has been most useful. Throughout my life I have had many instances in which I could have complained and given up. Growing up with an autistic brother, I struggled a lot with embarrassment or frustration. I sometimes wished for a "normal" brother. My dad made it very clear that I was not to be a victim, because I was lucky to have a brother like Jack. His "don't be a victim" speech stuck, because whenever I've been inclined to feel sorry for myself, I remember the speech.

When I was in fourth grade, my mom was diagnosed with breast cancer. Shortly after my mom recovered, I was diagnosed with a rare blood disorder and had a bone marrow transplant. I was sick for almost two years. I knew it was something I had to deal with, and did not want the pity of others. I did not complain that I was missing school and time with my friends, nor did I get upset that the hospital beds were uncomfortable. And now, after my dad died at such an early age, I do not feel like a victim. I believe it is unfair, but I do not blame anyone or anything for my loss. I appreciate every second I had with him, and because of my dad's lessons I am strong and motivated to keep living my life to the fullest.

Dear Daughters

JULIA WAS ONE OF SEVENTY-TWO graduates in the Convent of the Visitation's class of 2012. As winter was wearing out its welcome, she and I joined a group of mothers and daughters for spring break in Mexico.

Sitting by the pool one morning, I asked mothers who were keeping a watchful eye on sunbathing daughters if they would help me craft a column. With our daughters about to launch their independent lives, I asked, what words of wisdom would you want to impart? What do you wish you had known when you were in their stage of life? Our conversation led to one of my favorite columns.

*   *   *

Despite media reports of violence in Mexico, spring break was a memory maker spent with eight mothers and eight daughters indulging in the sun, surf, and sand in surprisingly quiet Playa del Carmen. We shopped in empty stores, enjoyed water aerobics, salsa dancing, watered-down exotic cocktails, and walks on the beach. We agreed that what happens in Mexico stays in Mexico, so further details will not be forthcoming.

But there is something we'd like to share. As we lounged by the beach, the moms reflected on what we wish we'd known when we were our daughters' age, what we now know, and what we'd like our girls to know. So, we offer counsel we could have used many decades ago; the reflections of mothers who have walked different paths but will launch our girls together with love and pride:

Dear Daughter,

The world has changed dramatically since you were born eighteen years ago. Three women have served as secretary of state and several have run for president. Terrorists attacked us on our own soil, so we pack our toiletries in ridiculously small plastic bags when we travel. We communicate on minuscule keyboards and multitask like mad. We have constant access to a worldwide web that connects you instantaneously to the cute guys you met in Mexico (oops!).

Soon you will leave the protective shelter of home and school. You might be stunned to learn how much it costs to support yourself, and that life as portrayed by reality TV shows is anything but that. As mothers, we cannot protect you from what we know to be reality: life will bring joy and pain, opportunities and obstacles. We have done our best to prepare you to navigate it all. But in case you've missed the lessons, we offer you this missive to carry in your minds and souls. If you should misplace it, we are always just a phone call—or a text—away.

The first year of college may be hard. You will need to figure out how to be a juggler—when to strive for moderation and when to push the limits. You will need to manage your time and your finances. It could take awhile to master the art of balancing laundry, exams, a social life, and maybe even a job. Be patient. Be resourceful. Be confident. Relish the empowerment that competence and independence breed.

You'll need to be your own advocate in ways you may not imagine right now. You might miss a deadline on a paper and need to negotiate with your professor. Your roommate might have nonstop visitors; your tiny abode might become a toxic wasteland. Don't suffer in silence, but be respectful. Respect is a two-way street.

Regardless of how it may appear, drinking is not an NCAA sport. No matter what others are doing, saying, or thinking, you will never regret making good choices. Be your own person, awkward as that may be. If you decide to drink, learn your tolerance. Use the buddy system. Relinquish your car keys. Many people have addictive tendencies, and you don't want to discover yours the messy way. Do you want to be one of those girls who slams shots, and ends the evening with mascara cascading down her face?

College can be a blast, but it can also be stressful. Whatever you are struggling with, you will get through it—and you need not face it alone. Take a risk and open up to others. When a friend or roommate is feeling blue, reach out. You might save a life.

There is a correlation between effort and outcome. Ninety-nine percent of anything is what you put into it. Push yourself. Work toward something you never thought you could do. Run a marathon. Choose a finish line and experience the exhilaration of crossing it. Dig deep and finish strong.

Choosing your major may be overwhelming. Take time to discover your passion and nurture it. Embrace your gifts. If you do what you are passionate about, you will find contentment. Everything else—money included—will work out. Keep an open mind. Many things you think could never happen do.

You are in the prime of your life. There are endless products and services to enhance your appearance, but it will change as you age. (You may have noticed that time and gravity aren't always kind to moms in swimsuits). Don't neglect your inner beauty; it is what will draw people in and truly define you. Be the go-to friend who is a good listener and protects others' confidences. Learn to accept and give compliments with grace and sincerity.

While you mostly communicate with digital devices, adults actually talk to one another. Explore the world. Read books. Study abroad. Sharing something you love makes you intriguing, exceptional, and desirable. Master the art of conversation by having something interesting to say.

And please call home.

With love, Mom

Time: Both Ally and Adversary

AFTER JACK LEFT boarding school in New Hampshire in the spring of 2010, he moved into an apartment near our home. Personal care attendants were responsible for helping him perform activities of daily living, such as cooking, cleaning, shopping, and exercising.

During the day, he attended a transition program called Branch Out. The school district's program was designed to bridge the education and employment worlds for students with challenges. At Branch Out, Jack developed a strong bond with his special education teacher, who was a welcome capstone to his educational experience. Exceedingly patient, Pat spent long hours with Jack, nurturing his creative tendencies. Though Jack continued to ignore punctuation and grammar rules, he filled pages with beautiful, romantic stories she edited for him.

With the clock ticking on the two-year transition program, the panic I felt when Julia was discharged from the hospital revisited me. The safety net I'd relied upon for close to two decades was being rolled up. My needy son's future rested totally in my hands. I found myself at the computer once again, this time writing for the *Huffington Post*.

* * *

Time can be our ally. It can also be our adversary. For months now I have been marking its passage with ever-growing dread. By June, our school district will have fulfilled its mandate to educate my son.

As its obligation is being extinguished, mine is being rekindled with great urgency. Despite exhaustive and costly efforts to socialize and educate him, Jack cannot manage the academic demands of college-level courses. He doesn't have the staying power for a full-time job because his attention span is short and his anxiety high. He's interested in people—but on his own (limited) terms.

We've investigated programs that would prepare him for employment by working a few hours a week at a light industrial concern, doing cleanup in a day treatment program, scanning documents, or putting items into bags or boxes. He could volunteer at the library or the food shelf. But those activities fall short of what I'd envisioned for him. Moreover, twenty-four hours are a stretch to fill when you have few interests and no friends to pass the time with.

Jack's future is no more predictable than any of ours. But about one thing I am certain. While my dream, my optimistic goal, is for him to live without supports and to become a taxpaying citizen, if that does not occur, I will remain by his side. I will guide him as he makes the decisions that are within his ability and put on my guardian hat when he needs me to do so.

. . .

My concerns weren't far off the mark. Since he exited the Branch Out program, Jack has spent his time in job training programs, but has not sought employment. Through a process of elimination, we are discerning what suits him, and what does not. He's become more verbal about his feelings and more aware of his limitations.

I fear that employment will be an ongoing challenge for him, with limited solutions. But I won't relinquish my dream that Jack will find a meaningful pursuit in life, for it is his dream, too. Though he struggles to identify what his work will look like, he reports that it feels good to have a purpose in life.

.

Impulse Buyer

DR. KAREN RITCHIE identified five types of creatures cancer patients may encounter on their journey: the preachers, the clueless, the bolters, the angels, and the fellow travelers. When I was going through my treatment in the summer of 2003, I encountered another type of creature: an impulse buyer.

As I was having poison pumped into my veins and fighting fatigue, Ted informed me that he and his brother Tom were going to purchase a boat. A boat? A friend of Tom's was being transferred, and he was having a fire sale on his pristine, twenty-five-foot cabin cruiser. The brothers decided to buy "their boat" together.

The boat was a battleground between Ted and me for quite a while. At a precarious time in my life, I felt I was being excluded. The boat was a big purchase, the kind of decision we would make together for our family. What was this "brothers boat" all about? Was this karma at work—payback for my unilateral decision to leave the workforce years earlier?

In hindsight, I see how the boat was a distraction for Ted during a frightening time. In the moment, though, it seemed like a peculiar purchase, and I was prickly that the decision didn't involve me.

With my health restored, the boat grew on me. With thirteen years between Julia and Caitie, it was challenging to find activities that would interest all the kids. And the boat offered us a peaceful place to unwind and socialize with our friends. We'd enjoy cocktails on board, followed by dinner at a local restaurant. We'd cruise the

•

river on peaceful evenings, our blood pressure dropping along with the setting sun.

Julia loved to take her friends out on the St. Croix River that separates Minnesota and Wisconsin. Ted would pull the kids on the tube for hours. Jack loved to go tubing, too, though sometimes he preferred to bury himself in a book in the cabin while others tubed, swam, or chilled.

In the summer of 2009, we planned for Dan, Nicole, Caitie, and Peter to come home for Ted's July 4th birthday. Everyone loved to go on the boat, but it was a bit tight for all of us. This time Ted consulted me. We agreed to buy two Jet Skis—his gift to himself, he said, for what turned out to be his last birthday.

The Jet Skis were as fun as we hoped they would be. We took turns racing each other up and down the river, our competitive natures surfacing. Even Jack took a turn at the controls, eyes focused directly in front of him as he motored straight up the river. I sat behind him, my arms wrapped around his waist and a smile stretching across my windblown face, as my head swirled, checking for traffic in the wings. The boat and Jet Skis provided welcome laughs and memories of our final family vacation together.

Shortly after Ted died, I sold the Jet Skis and my interest in the boat. I couldn't back up the boat when it was on the trailer. How would I maintain all those cylinders? Who would use them with me? Though the boat began as a friction point, it ultimately became a shared interest, the source of many great memories. It was many months before I could drive across the bridge that joins Minnesota and Wisconsin and turn my eye toward the marina where we'd kept the boat.

Grief and Joy

FOR MUCH OF THE YEAR before Julia left for college, I wallowed in anticipatory grief. She is my baby, the one whose life had been so tenuous. I have a bond with her that defies description. I dreaded the thought of her leaving, but I was mindful of my role. As her mother, I was responsible for giving her roots and wings. I'd done my best to give her roots. It was time to let her spread her wings.

In the same period of time, we celebrated Caitie's marriage to Peter, and Dan's to Nicole. Though little was said, I'm confident we shared the same sentiments: Life was marching on without the man who bound us, who coveted life's big moments. It was a bittersweet time filled with grief and joy.

Jack provided unexpected cheer at Caitie's wedding in Cabo San Lucas. With a breeze blowing and the waves breaking nearby, he declared he wanted to make a toast. And did he ever!

His long and poignant remarks left guests speechless and tearful. Jack congratulated Caitie and Peter, and urged them to "hurry up and have a baby . . . and to name it Ted."

Then he cautioned his new brother-in-law not to "do anything stupid."

Apparently, Caitie and Peter took his words to heart. In April 2014, we welcomed a new generation to our clan with the arrival of Theresa Grace Johnson. The baby we call Teddy is full of personality. Though she lives in Colorado, technology enables us to *almost* reach out and touch her. With her photo on my nightstand,

I open my eyes each morning to the baby girl who bears her grandpa's name, blue eyes, and infectious grin, ensuring I start each day with a smile.

When Dan became engaged, he asked Jack to be one of his groomsmen. I was deeply moved, but a bit concerned. I knew Dan and Nicole wanted their Arizona wedding to be perfect, and Jack can be a bit unpredictable at times. I questioned whether he would stand quietly for the duration of the lengthy Catholic ceremony, given his short attention span and tendency to yawn during church services.

He surprised us all. Looking very dashing in his tuxedo, his beard neatly trimmed by his brother, he handled himself with grace—and nary a yawn. But the minute the bride and groom walked down the aisle together, Jack began asking when he could change from the uncomfortable patent leather rentals to his worn-in tennis shoes.

Julia graduated from high school in 2012. We celebrated with family, friends, and great Mediterranean food. In mid-August, she and I loaded up my Toyota Highlander with a ridiculous number of shoes and sweaters. I couldn't fathom how she would fit so much stuff into her dorm room, but she was confident she could.

With a drizzling rain teasing our curly heads, we unloaded her boxes and clothes and successfully squeezed her belongings into her tiny abode. Then she gave me the sign. It was time for both of us to move on.

I drove west on Interstate 94 from Madison to St. Paul in a daze. When a state trooper pulled me over and asked why I was speeding, I could only offer the truth.

"I just dropped my daughter off at college."

Though Wisconsin state troopers are prone to pouncing on Minnesota motorists, Trooper Luck let me off with a warning.

With Julia in Madison, Caitie and Dan in Denver with their spouses, and Jack chilling in his bachelor pad, I felt untethered. Though Caitie and Dan assured me they wanted to remain a family,

I didn't know what that would look like or how much I should try to shape the future. We needed a substitute for the boat and the Jet Skis; something to bring us together. Perhaps it would be grandchildren.

My friend Liz often reminds me that many of her other friends struggle to realign relationships with their adult children. We baby boomers were very involved in our children's lives as they were growing up. They may, or may not, want the same level of involvement with us as adults—if they can even make time for us.

Regardless of whether they relocate, as Caitie and Dan did, our adult children are absorbed in their own lives. They have jobs, friends, significant others, and homes. When they marry, they join another family that has its own hopes and expectations. Add children to the mix, and even the tightest of families struggle to get their bearings.

It's a work in progress. I'm not certain how we will move forward. But I've lived my life with the belief that "where there's a will, there's a way." I'm optimistic that we will find our way to new traditions in this exciting phase of life.

part
eight

Daring
to Dream

Focused and Frustrated

FOR MUCH OF MY LIFE, I expected bad things to happen. They always had. Asked about my dreams or bucket list, I typically responded with a shrug or a blank stare. I was reluctant to get too hopeful about anything. On the rare occasions when I'd allowed myself to get excited about an adventure, my hopes were dashed.

When Julia underwent her bone marrow transplant, we spent the better part of a year in the hospital and outpatient bone marrow transplant clinic. I often chatted with her doctor, Margy MacMillan, during our visits. Margy is brilliant, beautiful, outgoing, and athletic. She often wears hot pink, a striking contrast to her shiny dark hair. Her infectious laugh frequently announces her arrival, proclaiming her capacity to maintain a sense of humor in the face of dire medical crises.

During one of Julia's outpatient visits, Margy mentioned she had been selected to be one of twenty-four cyclists to participate in the Bristol-Myers Squibb Tour of Hope Ride, along with Lance Armstrong. The grueling ride would begin in California on September 29, 2005, wind south through Texas, up the eastern seaboard, culminating in Washington, DC on October 7. Along the way, team members would share information about cancer research.

Though the select group would ride across the country, anyone could participate in a fundraising ride from Columbia, Maryland, to Washington, DC, where throngs of cancer survivors in yellow shirts would greet them.

I desperately needed a distraction from my nursing duties; I needed a goal beyond ensuring that my daughter would live.

I bought a road bike and began training. At the beginning of October, I boxed up my bike and flew to Washington, DC, where I met my brother Steve and my friend Pat. The three of us planned to ride the fifty miles together.

Then a stranger named Tammy intervened. With little warning, Tropical Storm Tammy struck Maryland and Washington, DC. With water rushing through the streets, ride organizers reluctantly canceled the fundraising ride from Columbia to Washington.

Led by Lance Armstrong, the team that included Julia's doctor rode into Washington, DC, for a soggy, anticlimactic finish. My bike remained in its box, unassembled, to be returned to Minnesota without a turn of the wheel.

I was crushed. For months afterward, I was angry and depressed. I'd set a goal. I had worked toward it. After everything I'd been through the previous years, why did it have to rain—pour—on *that* day?

There was a silver lining, though. I became hooked on riding. Ted and I became active members of our neighborhood cycling group, the Copperfield Clydesdales, comprised of middle-aged guys and me—"the pony." Over the years we logged many miles together, chatting and exploring the Twin Cities on two wheels.

By fall of 2009 I was ready to try a different kind of adventure. Focused on writing, but constantly interrupted by distractions at home, I coveted a writing retreat. As I deliberated over the idea, Ted intervened.

"Just do it," he said, frustrated by my indecision.

He gave me a budget and told me to take as much time as I needed. With Jack at boarding school in New Hampshire, he and Julia would be just fine without me.

In my deliberative style, I labored over the decision about where and when to go. I pictured a warm destination with water, which both soothes and motivates me. It would be a catalyst for creativity.

I also wanted to feel safe, but not isolated. I settled on Isla Mujeres, a small island close to Cancun, Mexico. My only concern was whether I would be too lonely if I spent thirteen days by myself. After all, I'd never lived alone.

Ted died thirty days before I was due to depart for Mexico. My trip washed away in one of the crashing waves of my grief, supplanted by more urgent tasks, such as rewriting my will and establishing a trust for Jack. I was too overwhelmed by my loss and my burgeoning duties to allow my thoughts to linger on the soothing waves I'd eagerly anticipated.

Turkish Delight

BY 2013 I was experiencing an unfamiliar phenomenon: I had no crisis in my life. Was this what life was like for other people? I was busy, but who wasn't? My stress was self-induced, a function of a fast-paced world driven by technology.

With Julia attending college in Wisconsin and Jack living in his own apartment, I was surprisingly comfortable sharing my home with Chuck: my four-legged companion who shadowed me, ate on a schedule, lived for his walks, and shed like crazy. But I was also itching for adventure.

When my friends Chris and Dan invited me to sail with them on their fifty-five-foot sailboat, I accepted with relish. The gorgeous blue-and-green water in the Turkish Riviera was alluring, the perfect setting for a relaxing getaway. But I couldn't go to Turkey without exploring Istanbul.

The invitation came long before officials in Syria acknowledged the presence of chemical weapons. It preceded discussions about retaliation against a country only a few hundred miles to the east of my destination. As those developments unfolded, I debated whether to proceed with my extraordinary "use it or lose it" opportunity.

The lure of the sea prevailed. Casting aside worries about potential situations over which I had no control, I plunged out of my comfort zone and pressed ahead with plans to fly to Istanbul and tour the city alone before joining my friends on their boat.

In late September, I left for Istanbul. The trip began badly when I missed my connecting flight in London due to a weather delay in Chicago. The details of hours spent making other arrangements are too exhausting to recall, much less to report. Suffice it to say, I arrived in Istanbul thirty-six hours after I left home, hundreds of dollars poorer and completely unraveled.

Having cleared customs shortly before midnight, I watched my reticent driver leave the airport and merge into a swarm of lights and activity reminiscent of Las Vegas. Imagined dangers yielded to real challenges. Though I had worried about bombings at airports, I had not anticipated the stress of not understanding one word of a language spoken by people who looked and sounded nothing like me.

The young man in the front seat of the taxi looked like most I encountered during my two weeks in the foreign land. He had dark hair and eyes and spoke a language I couldn't understand. Yet when his cellphone came to life, I discovered that even Turkish men appreciate George Thorogood's distinctly Western tune, "Bad to the Bone."

I was relieved when English-speaking staff greeted me at a cozy hotel. After a good night's sleep, I indulged in a Turkish bath; an amazing experience unlike any I've encountered elsewhere. A man who was obviously well experienced in doing so, lathered, scrubbed, and rinsed the stress right out of my body. It was delightful.

I planned to spend time in various parts of the city that spans two continents before I joined Chris and Dan to celebrate my birthday on their sailboat. Refreshed by my Turkish bath, I set out on foot with an unknown destination, but a map in hand.

Predominantly Muslim but with a secular government, Turkey felt like a man's country. Day and night, men traveled in pairs or groups, playing backgammon and sipping coffee in cafes. I rarely spotted women without male companions. My solo travel was not the norm.

Tourists flock to the historic part of Istanbul. Well-preserved palaces and mosques, decorated with hand-sewn silk carpets and crystal chandeliers, are monuments to long-ago traditions in which sultans shared quarters with their wives, mothers, and harems.

The Grand Bazaar features three thousand shops spread over sixty streets. Sounds, colors, textures, and smells captivate the senses. The world's largest covered market attracts more than ninety-one million visitors each year.

Though we didn't speak the same language, proprietors had their ways of soliciting my business. Owners or employees, always male, stood in the doorway, or outside their establishments, imploring me to purchase a cappuccino or peruse their carpets.

Competition for sales of jewelry, carpets, handmade clothing, and souvenirs was intense. Prices were rarely posted. Though guidebooks explained that bartering is the norm, some proprietors seemed to relish the practice—while others took offense at it.

Navigating the indoor shopping area was a full contact sport, for which the rules were unclear. My best defense against an aggressive offensive was to avoid eye contact, maintain an arm's length distance, and enter an establishment only if I intended to part with my Turkish lira.

The Blue Mosque, constructed between 1603 and 1617, is one of the final structures of Ottoman religious architecture. I was walking toward it when an older gentleman approached me and offered to give me a tour at no charge. In clear English, he explained he was a retired teacher who currently worked in his family's carpet business. He was direct and seemingly harmless, so I accepted his offer.

As we walked rapidly toward the mosque, my guide offered a fascinating account of its history. When we arrived, he elbowed past tourists as he explained we needed to remove our shoes when we entered. Though I'd expected to spend a fair amount of time in the exquisite building, my guide had a different agenda. In less time than it had taken to walk there, he offered an overview of its history, then steered me toward the exit.

Once he'd directed me out of the building, he revealed his true motivation. As my eyes struggled to adjust to the bright sunlight, the squat older man posed a question he assumed I anticipated.

"Now do you want to go see my family's carpets?"

Feeling foolish and betrayed, I declined—repeatedly—until my "guide" departed in a huff, likely in search of his next prey.

Istanbul was fascinating, educational, historic, exhausting, and rich with lessons. When I stepped off the airplane in Dalaman, it was immediately apparent that the second phase of my adventure would be quite different from the first. As I anticipated, the sunshine, sea air, and comfort of friends allowed me to decompress and experience Turkey at a much less frenetic pace.

As I settled into the rhythm of life on the boat—no noise, deadlines, or crowds—I felt like a different woman. With my friends as my guides, I saw a different side of the same country.

We strolled through Gocek and Fethiye. We indulged in a communal Turkish bath in Fethiye that strained my modesty. We climbed to the top of historic Gemiler Island, and took in the expansive view of our surroundings. Chris served healthy breakfasts and lunches on board. At night we left the boat and enjoyed savory meals at local establishments.

With many British vacationers present in the coastal towns, English was no longer such a foreign language. Though shopkeepers and café owners solicited customers, they were less intense than their counterparts in Istanbul. The blue water of the aptly named Turquoise Coast was stunning. We saw fishing boats and yachts and gullets—the Turkish yachts favored by tourists.

In a week's time, my hectic tourist's pace ceded to the undemanding schedule on a vessel with no definite destination. The soothing, rocking motion of the sea and companionship of easygoing hosts who spoke my language returned me to my comfort zone. I discovered my version of Turkish Delight.

Starkey Cares

GROWING UP on a Missouri farm, Bill Austin dreamed of making a difference in the world. When he heard about Albert Schweitzer, a medical missionary whose work in Africa earned him a Nobel Prize, Bill was inspired to follow a similar path.

Bill moved to Minnesota in 1967 and purchased a business he named Starkey Hearing Technologies. He chose a slogan for his company that endures decades later: "So the world may hear." With Bill's ability to match people with hearing aids, the Eden Prairie business became one of the top-five hearing technology companies in the world, with factories in twenty-eight countries.

His passion also gave birth to the Starkey Hearing Foundation. The foundation's purpose is to provide hearing to people who cannot afford it. To date, the foundation has traveled to more than one hundred countries and donated more than one million hearing aids, most provided by Starkey Hearing Technologies. Its next goal is to deliver an additional million devices in this decade through a global network of care.

When Bill met his wife Tani, it was like a hand finding its glove. Both from humble backgrounds, they have a shared work ethic and passion for helping others to hear. As cofounder of the foundation, Tani manages the big picture so Bill can focus on his passion. "Bill understands business, works like a farmer, has a missionary's heart, and understands money." For Bill, it's never been about the money, his wife says. His focus is on delivering hearing to anyone who wants to be in the hearing world.

The Starkey office walls are lined with photographs of icons—politicians, actors, musicians, and athletes—who purchased Starkey hearing aids. Recognizing their gratitude and the value of their networks, Tani invited some of their best customers to a gala in 2001. Eight hundred people attended the inaugural event, which raised $600,000. She was onto something big.

More than a decade later, the annual red carpet gala in St. Paul draws celebrities from around the world, honors hands-on philanthropists, such as actor Forest Whitaker, and raises millions of dollars. The net proceeds from the gala help to fund the missions.

When I met them shortly before the 2014 gala, Tani and Bill had recently returned to Minnesota. They had spent much of the year on mission trips around the world. Late in the afternoon, the Starkey offices were bustling with activity, even though it was a Friday (which for many Minnesotans is time to head to the cabin).

Tani and I spoke for more than an hour. She captivated me with her seemingly boundless energy and passion for her work. As we said our good-byes, she asked if I wanted to attend the gala the following weekend. A week later, my daughter and I enjoyed an amazing Sunday evening.

The gala was a contagious celebration of good works and good will. It began with Lee Greenwood singing "God Bless the USA." As the song wound down, guests looked up to see a bald eagle traversing the darkened room. During a five-hour dinner filled with music and stories about the international efforts of Starkey and its honorees, guests bid substantial sums to go on mission trips.

After I attended the gala, I thought about some of the most poignant sounds in my life: my children's first cries as they entered the world; the "I do's" when my stepchildren and their spouses exchanged wedding vows; and the mournful wail of bagpipes at my husband's funeral. I'm blessed to have hearing that allows me to experience not only sounds, but also the lumps in the throat that occasionally accompany them.

But several hundred million men, women, and children don't share that gift. While not deaf, they have experienced debilitating hearing loss due to undiagnosed ear infections, trauma, aging, tumors, loud music, explosions, and more. Their hearts don't race when tornado sirens warn us to take cover. They don't sprout goose bumps when the first notes of *Pachelbel's Canon* herald a bride's walk down the aisle.

The Austins animate their mantra "alone we can't do much, but together we can change the world." In the first half of 2014, they visited fourteen countries and fitted 35,000 people with donated hearing aids. In July, they held a mission at corporate headquarters, fitting many people with special needs. With additional missions scheduled for China, Africa, Afghanistan, the Philippines, and more, they were on track to surpass the 165,000 devices they had fitted in 2013.

Mission success depends on partnering with local organizations, like Rotary Club, that identify people with hearing problems. Once there, Starkey teams follow an action plan of screening recipients, fitting the hearing aids, and providing aftercare. They train locals to ensure patients use the equipment properly. And they make return visits.

For Bill and Tani, the missions are a hands-on experience in which they are very involved with the people they are fitting. Tani explains they've got about two seconds for the person to trust them and believe they're going to help them. They are providing more than just a hearing aid. "We're giving them respect, asking their names, looking them in the eye, and shaking their hands. And we're doing it personally."

The result is virtually tangible. Tani describes how they can almost see people fill with sound. "They will sit there as you try the hearing aids on, and all of a sudden their eyes will pop. It's like a light switch."

I was struck by the way in which the Austins focus on opportunities, not obstacles. With so much emphasis on what is wrong with the world, Tani says, they try to show what is good in it. "Take the pioneers. If they had focused on what they would have to overcome they wouldn't have done it . . . It's pretty incredible what we've been able to do in such a short time with so many partners, by thinking like the pioneers. Not thinking about why you shouldn't do it—just by doing it."

Hearing Aids and Helping Hands

THE GALA FESTIVITIES didn't end with dinner and entertainment. Julia and I ran into Paul and Destini Molitor at the gala after-party. The Minnesota Twins manager and his wife had participated in a Starkey mission in the Dominican Republic and were inspired by the Austins' work.

Destini and I serve on the Women's Impact Foundation board together, but Julia knew little about the Molitors, other than that Paul had been a professional baseball player. Struggling to make conversation, my twenty-year-old said to the baseball Hall of Famer, "The Paul Molitor burger at the Nook (a St. Paul eatery) is my favorite." We all shared a chuckle.

Not long after the gala, Tani sent an email with photographs of Julia and me with the Molitors. At the bottom of the email, I spotted an intriguing postscript: "Would you and your daughter like to go on a mission to Peru in two weeks?" We would travel to Cajamarca, via Lima, the third week of August. When we'd completed our work we would fly to Cusco, the launching point for a day trip to Machu Picchu.

Julia would start her junior year at the University of Wisconsin-Madison just after Labor Day, but she was free until then. I had an unusually open schedule. Could it be that easy? Did I dare to dream again?

Armed with assorted medications, Julia and I joined the group in Cajamarca, a city of more than 200,000 in northwestern Peru.

Starkey staff, led by the Austins, arrived with hearing aids and seemingly unlimited energy. Mission sponsors came from various cities in the United States and Canada. With a common purpose, we settled into an easy rhythm, sharing pointers and translators.

Starkey partners in Peru had identified men, women, and children with hearing loss. The team arrived with hundreds of quality hearing aids of varying power levels to be fitted into pre-made molds. On each of the four mornings we spent in Cajamarca, we arrived at the local university to find men, women, and children waiting expectantly to go through a well-established process. I'd anticipated more children than adults, but the opposite was true. Rows of plastic chairs were set up in the gymnasium, separating the fitting section from the area where individuals had their ears checked and cleaned. Many people sat quietly for hours, waiting for a local Rotary Club volunteer to direct them to a fitting chair.

As fitters, our job was to select a hearing aid that provided the optimal power level and was set at the best volume. Some of the mission sponsors were professionals who fit their clients with hearing aids every day, using the latest technology. We used a behavioral approach, leaning into the individual's ear and repeating "*ba ba ba*," as we raised or lowered the volume.

Many of the people we fitted were fatigued. Some, given their age, likely suffered from some degree of senility; so it was difficult at times to discern whether the hearing aid was effective. But facial expressions were revealing. The upward turn of lips meant we'd made contact; a grimace indicated the volume was too loud. Interpreters helped to clarify whether we had hit the sweet spot. While they all wanted the gift Starkey had brought to town, not everyone was fitted successfully. And that was hard.

A variety of factors caused hearing loss. For some it was aging; others had experienced trauma from accidents or from working in the local mines. Many worked the land, for we were in dairy farm country. The years in the sun were evidenced by the Peruvians' gnarled, weathered hands and deeply lined faces, though they wore enormous hand-woven hats, made of trimmed leaves of palm trees. The women were often harder to fit than the men, mostly due to long, coarse hair that had to be adjusted in order to place the hearing aids behind their ears.

One morning, a ninety-eight-year-old woman named Maria approached my station with her two daughters. Maria had significant hearing loss, as did one daughter. I later learned the daughters had been caring for Maria since she lost her hearing at age seventy-five and were frustrated by her inability to hear them. The women had learned of the Starkey mission and surprised their mother by taking her to Cajamarca. They rode for eight hours on a bus with no bathroom.

I fitted Maria first; then someone found a plastic chair for the matriarch while she waited for her daughter. As I fitted her daughter, I could see Maria chatting with the Starkey videographer, who happened to be fluent in Spanish. She was animated, grateful, and delighted she would finally be able to hear her twenty-eight grandchildren speak.

Later, I fitted a young schoolboy who was shy and nervous, and reluctant to make eye contact. When I tickled him to get him to smile for the photographer, he surprised me with an adorable set of dimples. With hearing aids in both of his ears, I suspect those dimples might surface more often.

Across the room from me, a hearing instrument specialist from New York fitted a little girl who had never heard her own voice before. Suddenly, the room erupted with what initially sounded like a child crying. In fact, it was the girl who was missing two front teeth. She was experimenting, joyfully, with the voice she'd just discovered.

A fitting typically ended with hugs, some kisses, and profuse thanks and blessings, after we had placed a plastic medal around the recipient's neck and pronounced him or her a "campeon." Occasionally I would forget to place the medal around my new acquaintance's neck. I knew people had been waiting for hours and was trying to work as quickly as possible. If I forgot, the man, woman, or child returned for the plastic medal—a prized possession, regardless of age or gender.

Everyone worked long hours, but no one more so than Bill and Tani. They are wealthy people who could easily retire and spend their days with their grandchildren. Yet they choose to spend most of the year on mission trips because they are devoted to making the world a better place, one person at a time.

We began each day with a huddle, a cheer, and a reminder from Bill to make it a beautiful day. I'd like to think, for the nearly 1,300 people we helped in that short week, we did just that.

Cleft Lips and Courage

NOT LONG AFTER the Starkey gala, I was honored to be one of thirty Minnesota "women of note" at a Children's Hospital Association luncheon. Kim Valentini was another woman of note. In 2003 Kim founded Smile Network International, a nonprofit that serves much the same population as the Starkey Foundation by providing cleft lip and palate surgeries at no cost to the families. I introduced myself and told Kim I'd like to write about her work. We met for coffee, then for wine, then for a walk, our chance encounter blossoming into a friendship.

Though the organization has garnered media attention since its inception, Kim was eager to have a writer share a firsthand account. She invited me to accompany Smile Network on a mission trip to Cusco, Peru, in November 2014.

I knew little about cleft lips and palates before I met Kim. Most American babies born with cleft lips (an opening in the upper lip) or cleft palates (a hole in the roof of the mouth) have surgeries before their first birthdays, so it is rare to see the disfiguring birth defects in the United States. In countries like Peru, India, Haiti, and Vietnam, clefts often remain uncorrected by families who cannot afford the elective surgery. Consequently, children have difficulty eating and gaining weight. Food passes through the open palate and exits the nose. They develop ear infections and dental problems, and struggle with speech.

A native of Minnesota, Kim left a successful corporate marketing and public relations career because she was looking for something more . . . a way to have a greater impact and to see more of the world. She'd whetted her appetite for helping children with cleft lips and palates while serving on the board of a physician-run nonprofit that performs surgeries around the world. She founded Smile Network to provide the same service with a different model.

With fewer than a handful of full-time staff and a large network of donors and volunteers, ranging from farmers to Delta Airlines, Smile Network has performed more than three thousand surgeries in dozens of countries. The work is gratifying, not only because of the physical changes the surgeries produce, but also for the social impact.

As I interviewed mothers, my translator and I struggled to remain composed. Their stories were incredible and heart breaking.

When Fabrizio was born, his father refused to accept him as his child. Taking their thirteen-year-old son, he left the baby, his wife, and their six-year-old daughter because he believed an archaic fallacy that his son was evil, or cursed.

Samuel was born in early 2014, about the same time as Fabrizio. His cleft lip and palate made it so difficult for him to eat and gain weight he had to be hospitalized in Cusco, about an hour bus ride from their home. For a month, his mother, Ricardina, left home before sunrise each day to travel to the hospital, where she pumped her breast milk and held her newborn. Late in the evening, she returned home.

In July, Smile Network conducted a mission in Cusco. Both Ruth and Ricardina took their baby boys to be screened. Neither met the ten-pound weight requirement. Both mothers were encouraged to try again when the surgical team returned in the fall. It was particularly difficult for Kim Valentini to turn Samuel away because she didn't know if the six-month-old, six-pound baby boy would survive, much less gain four more pounds in as many months.

Ricardina was determined to return with Samuel, but she faced additional obstacles when her husband was seriously injured at work and hospitalized in Lima. Her seventeen-year-old daughter dropped out of school to support the family, and her fourteen-year-old son took care of his younger siblings when Ricardina went to Lima to visit their father.

With his mother's attention diverted, Samuel's health deteriorated. He was hospitalized again, this time close to their rural home. Doctors predicted Samuel would die and discouraged Ricardina from pursuing the cleft lip surgery. Ignoring those who tried to dissuade her, Ricardina transferred Samuel to a Cusco hospital and initiated an aggressive feeding schedule.

When Smile Network returned to Cusco in November, both Ruth and Ricardina took their baby boys to the mission site. Spotting Kim Valentini, the weary mother held Samuel up, one weathered hand under each tiny arm. Though she speaks no English, she was able to say, "4.4 kilograms." When it was Samuel's turn for screening, many waited anxiously, for the "failure-to-thrive baby" had a large cheering section. Many pairs of eyes were moist when the pediatrician cleared him for surgery.

The days I spent in the Cusco hospital reinforced my belief that everything in life is relative. As I examined the conditions, I thought about the hospitals in which I've spent so much time, particularly with my daughter. I realized how great our medical care is and how lucky we've been, even under extraordinarily trying circumstances.

I recalled how, before Julia was admitted to the hospital for her bone marrow transplant, we toured the floor where patients remained in isolation for extended periods. Some rooms were small, maybe eight by ten, or ten by ten feet. Larger rooms contained medical equipment for patients who had more complex medical needs.

On admission day, Julia was escorted to the smallest room. It contained a standard hospital bed and nightstand, a Naugahyde chair that converted into a single bed, and a TV hanging from the wall. We had no idea how long we'd be calling this home, but it was not what we'd had in mind.

I complained to the nurse about the size of our room—like a petulant hotel guest expecting more upscale accommodations—then reached out to our friend, Dr. Dan Saltzman, to see if he could secure a larger room for us. The head of pediatric surgery, a cancer researcher, husband, and father of two, Dan has a very full plate. As I share this anecdote, I realize how inconsequential the size of Julia's room was. I'm embarrassed to have ever bothered Dan about it, as if he were the concierge at a luxury hotel.

Our hospital experience revisited me when we walked into the facility where Smile Network volunteers would operate on more than fifty kids in three-and-a-half days (with a fair number of medical staff and volunteers suffering from altitude sickness).

When families arrived at the Cusco hospital on screening day, they were directed to wooden benches to wait their turn. Some spent long hours waiting to learn whether their children would be among the lucky ones to be screened. I thought of all the doctors' offices, clinics, and hospitals in which I've spent a good portion of my adult life. Those facilities were furnished with carpet and comfortable chairs and stocked with magazines, children's books, daily newspapers, and televisions to occupy minds and time. They offer complimentary coffee, tea, and water for parched lips or a needed caffeine boost. Hospitals are staffed with Child Family Life specialists who prepare children for frightening procedures and entertain their siblings while parents meet with physicians.

In contrast, the Smile Network doctors performed surgeries in small rooms, using donated equipment, supplies, and medicine that volunteers had transported from the United States. When surgeries ended, volunteers took patients across the hall to a recovery room shared with other hospital patients. Beds came with no sheets, so Smile Network nurses used plastic bed covers (once on each side), wiping off the bloodstains left by the first patient before placing another on the bed.

When children were ready to leave the recovery room, volunteers took them out to the waiting room where mothers, fathers, siblings, and grandparents waited anxiously to see their loved one's corrected lip or palate. A translator explained what had occurred and what would happen next. Family members were escorted to the fourth floor ward as soon as a working elevator was available. In one room, beds were lined up side by side, with just enough room for a physician or parent to stand in between them. Most beds were shared by two small children, wrapped in their donated fleece blankets and whatever belongings the family had brought along.

Mothers—strangers just a day before—comforted crying babies, as nurses, doctors, and volunteers elbowed their way through the tiny room. The mothers shared the same fears, hope, relief, and concern about how to care for their children at home once the Americans had left Cusco. Some parents spent the night without food or blankets to warm themselves.

Exhausted, they left early the next morning to resume lives that were challenging without a child with a cleft lip or palate. With the cleft lips repaired, how would life be different? Would the neighbors and family members who had shunned them have a change of heart? Or would they always view the baby who had been born with a misshapen mouth as a devil child who bore bad tidings?

Dr. Raj Sarpal is a Minneapolis anesthesiologist who has gone on more than fifty medical missions, most of them with Smile Network. As the medical mission coordinator, he is responsible for ensuring that both patients and volunteers are healthy, as well as for scheduling all of the surgeries. Raj says nobody understands the value of these opportunities better than a boy who grew up in India.

The anesthesiologist uses his vacation time to present underprivileged children with a chance to integrate into society, obtain work, and have families. "Without this simple procedure, many of these children are relegated to back rooms of their homes, hidden from the public and, occasionally, their own families, without hope of ever having a meaningful life."

Pasta, Sweaters, and Smiles

SMILE NETWORK INTERNATIONAL'S MANTRA is "It takes $500 and forty-five minutes to change a life." Securing funding for thousands of cleft lip and palate surgeries, for impoverished patients around the world, is an ongoing effort. Many volunteers contribute time and money in a variety of fundraising initiatives to engage donors at all income levels. It's not uncommon for volunteers to become enamored with the work and the people. Kim exudes passion for the work and it is contagious.

Frank Marchionda owns I Nonni, an Italian restaurant just south of St. Paul. In 2007 a Smile Network volunteer stopped by his restaurant to ask whether he would contribute to the upcoming gala. She was hoping for a bottle of wine or a gift certificate. Frank declined. He and his wife Karen had already decided to become involved with Smile Network, and they wanted to participate on a much larger scale.

A tradition was born. Every year Frank closes I Nonni for one night to host what Kim describes as "an intimate, feel-good event with fabulous food and camaraderie." Frank's family and employees work the event for free. Frank's employees even donate their tips. Since 2007 the annual dinners, as well as cooking classes and smaller dinners I Nonni donates, have raised more than $350,000.

Frank plays a big role in raising funds over the course of the night. He says that when it comes to asking for money for Smile Network, he is "pretty much a lady of the evening." His strategy is to get the heartstrings going, then hit his guests up for money.

Since Smile Network places a premium on volunteers' time and money, it awards the nonmedical spots on mission trips to top volunteers and donors, or to gala guests who bid on them.

Kim invited the Marchiondas to go on a mission so they could see the magnitude of what they'd done. Frank resisted because he felt the money could be better spent on surgeries.

But Kim prevailed. Frank and Karen, a retired nurse, have gone on missions to Lima, Peru, and to a remote area in Kenya. On the first mission, husband and wife worked directly with the patients. On the second mission, Frank served a different role. Instead of spending time with the children, as he had during the first trip, he brought his culinary skills to the table. With the closest restaurant seventy-file miles away, he managed the kitchen while his wife helped with patients. Preparing food that had been shipped in advance from home, Frank served thirty volunteers three fabulous meals a day for ten days.

Judy Sunderman and Kim Hammes of Le Sueur, Minnesota, found their way to Smile Network through its adventure travel program, which participants pay for themselves. They were lured in by the opportunity to go on an adventure and to support a compelling need. In 2013 they hiked the Inca Trail; in 2014 they explored Ecuador by horseback. After each adventure, they joined the mission team, helping with families and managing medical records.

The Inca trek was an amazing experience. For four days, Sherpas carried their gear on their backs and cooks prepared meals. A Peruvian guide led the way, sharing his country's history. After navigating the 52,000-step trail, they reached Machu Picchu, one of the Seven Wonders of the World. The guide said, "The first day of the trek will be easy, the second challenging, the third beautiful, and the last amazing." The same could be said of my experience on the medical mission.

Before they participated in the missions, the Minnesota women, long-time friends and neighbors, began raising money. No effort was too small. They wrote letters soliciting contributions. Kim took donations at her Zumba class. A nephew raised $500 at his lemonade stand.

But their big event was the Ugly Sweater Ball. Determined to put the fun in fundraiser, they reached out to the residents of Le Sueur and neighboring Henderson, south of Minneapolis, and invited them to put on their ugly sweaters and spend a fun-filled evening at the Henderson Event Center. On a night in November 2013, they raised $16,000 and piqued the interest of the community.

A year later, they hosted the "Even Uglier Sweater Ball" a week after returning from the Cusco mission. They created interest and kept friends and supporters engaged through social media while they were in Peru, sharing updates and photos.

On the Saturday after Thanksgiving, local radio hosts joined other locals who filled VIP tables and bid hundreds of dollars as local celebrities modeled their ugly sweaters. By the end of the evening, they'd raised $28,000. Word of their efforts spread. After the event, three donors contributed an additional $25,000. With a combined population of fewer than 5,000, the people of Le Sueur and Henderson raised more than $50,000 to fund one hundred new smiles.

Several of us made the fifty-three-mile drive from Minneapolis to Henderson to attend the fundraiser. As Kim Valentini spoke about the organization, greeted guests, and personally thanked donors, I sensed a movement was afoot.

Everyone who purchased a bottle of wine in the wine pull, bid on donated and decorated Christmas trees, or bought raffle tickets for the ninety-nine bottles of beer display, was taking ownership, in small measure, of the smiles of children they will never meet.

Their involvement with Smile Network has been life changing, Judy says. Her husband, John, concurs. A farmer, he is eager to join his wife on a mission trip when his schedule permits. The impact has extended beyond the Sunderman and Hammes families. Judy described it as a big heart opening for the community. "People who contributed may never travel outside of the country, but they can feel like they went along. They made a difference in many children's lives tonight. And vice versa."

One of the Seven Wonders of the World

BOTH MISSION TRIPS TO PERU offered the opportunity to visit Machu Picchu. That was a big draw, especially for my adventurous daughter. But midweek during our Starkey mission trip in August, Julia became ill. By late Friday, having flown from Cajamarca to Cusco, elevation twelve thousand feet, we both felt dreadful.

We set our alarm for 3:00 a.m. Saturday, hoping to rally so we could join the Starkey group for the quick day trip. But weak and woozy from Cusco's elevation, we reluctantly concluded we didn't have the stamina or the stomach for the journey. Instead of joining the others, we spent the day in bed.

I flashed back to the Tour of Hope ride that was literally washed out; the Mexico writing retreat that never materialized because Ted died three weeks before I was scheduled to depart; and the tour to Ephesus, Turkey, that I paid for but never experienced because my driver purportedly went to fetch me at the wrong hotel. But I was too ill to nurse the memories. Moreover, I sensed another opportunity was on the horizon—at least for me, if not for Julia—and one day I'd make the trek to Machu Picchu.

Three months later, Smile Network turned the tide on my luck. When Kim invited me to go on the Peruvian mission, she explained that it would culminate in a trip to Machu Picchu. A second chance. It was meant to be.

Many adventure seekers make a four-day trek on the 52,000-stair Inca trail to reach Machu Picchu. Our route was far less taxing. It was a beautiful November day when we boarded the train for the first leg of our journey. Maureen Cahill, Smile Network's executive director, had invited a videographer and producer along to take photographs and video footage.

We left the town of Oilantaytambo, outside of Cusco, making our way up the mountainside to Aquas Calientes, where we joined our guide aboard a bus, traversing hairpin turns as we ascended 2,000 feet.

Located 8,000 feet above sea level, Machu Picchu is a popular tourist attraction that was hidden for centuries and rediscovered by an American archaeologist in 1919. Reportedly constructed around 1400 AD as an estate for an Incan ruler, the area was abandoned during the Spanish conquest of the Incan empire.

The ruins extend over a ridge in the Andes Mountain, with the Urumbaba River flowing below, weaving through the verdant valleys. Distant mountain tops nestled inside fluffy clouds that later released an afternoon shower.

Remnants of plazas, shrines and temples, baths and water systems populate the abandoned site. Masonry work consists of intricately fitted stones with openings interspersed throughout, offering a breathtaking view of the terraced hillside, on which crops were irrigated and grown.

The majestic landscape prompted many questions. How had the workers built the structures centuries ago without electricity, trains, or motorized vehicles to transport people and supplies? How many workers had it taken to build all the structures? Why had the inhabitants abandoned such an exquisite setting?

The capacity of human beings to stretch, accommodate, and adapt has endured, generation after generation. If the Incans could build a community high in the Andes Mountains, with none of the tools we take for granted today, then isn't virtually anything possible?

As I surveyed the mountains and valleys, it struck me that my life was on a new trajectory. For years, I felt as if I was perpetually balancing boulders on each shoulder. The boulders have finally rolled off, lightening my load considerably. They are where they rightly belong—among others that form the majestic view of Machu Picchu.

Billions of people share this planet. Many have experienced hardships far greater than mine. Few will have the chance to travel to a foreign country with amazing people, as I did, not once, but twice in 2014. Standing on the mountaintop surveying the splendor of one of the Seven Wonders of the World, I felt a rush of pride and satisfaction. I'd faced many obstacles, pushed myself to new heights. My life has been confusing, exhausting, frustrating, and at times surreal. But I've endured. I am a family crisis survivor. And I am blessed.

Epilogue

March 20, 2015, Ponte Verde Beach, Florida

I'm lying in bed, listening to the waves outside my window. My sister is lying in the bed next to me, in a restless slumber. We're at the beach with friends who are so close to my heart, the line between friends and family often blurs.

In the three decades since Ted introduced us, our respective families have fractured through divorce and death and reconfigured through marriage and birth. Yet the bonds remain and grow.

After Ted died, John and Sonya told me that my family was now their family. True to their word, they've remembered us on birthdays and holidays, included us in their weddings, and attended ours.

Thanks to John and Sonya, Caitie and Dan are also here with their spouses and my granddaughter Teddy. We've got a few empty seats, though. Julia is studying abroad in Ireland. She's also traveled to other countries, experiencing the world through her twenty-one-year-old eyes. I'm experiencing her adventures vicariously, with a heart that overflows with joy. Thanks to her brother, a fabulous medical team, and God's grace, her bone marrow transplant worked. She is exploring the world with a smile on her face.

Jack is content, living in his bachelor pad. He is a proud uncle who looks at photos of his niece Teddy in awe, chastising me for taking my eyes off of her before he does. He's trying to find the right training program or job to suit his skills and challenges. It's not easy. But we're not giving up.

●

Those of us who gathered in Florida are celebrating a wedding, a sixtieth birthday, and an exciting birth announcement. In a few months, my blended family will grow again. Dan and his wife Nicole are expecting twins.

As I listen to the waves outside my window, I'm struck by how differently I think of them now. Five years after I unexpectedly joined the freakin' widows club, the crashing waves arrive less frequently, typically at predictable junctures. My grief has found its place. It's ever present, but not immobilizing. New life has summoned new joy, a welcome antidote to sadness.

With Caitie and Dan living in Denver and spending time with their other family members, our holiday traditions are changing. Instead of sharing Christmas cheer, we've gathered in the Colorado mountains in the summertime. We can share meals, snuggle babies, and engage in a rousing game of Catch Phrase anytime, anywhere.

Other families have reached out to Jack, Julia, and me, setting places for us at their holiday dinner tables. We're grateful to be included. Once again, friends feel more like family.

I've gone full circle on my career, as I've made my way back to my roots in journalism. I've stepped away from the wall, emboldened by a writing platform that enables me to meet interesting people who are eager to share their stories and their adventures. I relish my role as a storyteller. I am deeply grateful to have discovered the healing power of words.

My writing and speaking have led me to one stranger after another who found the mettle to face challenges and embrace opportunities. Their energy, passion, and commitment have been contagious. I've reconciled with a practical, but optimistic, approach to life: hope for the best, but plan for the inevitable.

I'm relishing a second act that has no script. For the time being, my dog Chuck and I share the home I purchased in 2013. Though it feels like a transition home, who's to say? I have no idea who or what tomorrow will bring, or the day after tomorrow, or next year. I do know that I have a pocket full of wisdom, and a reliable support system to deal with whomever, or whatever, comes my way.

Regardless of the challenges, I remain mindful of the choice: *Bitter or Better.*

Acknowledgments

On a sunny day in June 2007 I was inspired to write an essay about life with a child with autism. Because Mike Burbach, editor of the St. Paul *Pioneer Press,* decided to run the essay, 700 words opened the door to a new chapter in my life. Eight years and more than 150 columns later, I am grateful to Mike for not only giving me the opportunity and the platform, but also for helping me to find my voice.

Writing this book without the benefit of my husband Ted's perspective and recall has been difficult. I've found an unexpected surrogate in our daughter Julia, who has offered thoughtful and candid feedback and reminders about details I'd overlooked or forgotten. My sister Traci and brothers Steve and Chris patiently fielded questions about our childhood, filling in gaps in my recall.

Author Vince Flynn provided encouragement when the book was still a concept. Hearing from an international bestseller that I had the skills to write a book was humbling and inspiring. I'm grateful for his support, saddened he did not live to see *Bitter or Bitter* come to life.

I'm thankful to everyone who read the manuscript and offered feedback and testimonials: Tani Austin, Pat Bailey, Mike Burbach, Traci Chadbourne, Rich Chapman, Carol Connolly, Molly Cox, Diane Cross, Jonah Goldberg, Maggie Gonring, Sona Mehring, Steve Ochse, Mary Treacy O'Keefe, Peg Schneeman Reagan, Amy Ronneberg, Dr. Dan Saltzman, Julia Sullivan, Therese Sullivan, Kevin Warren, Lee Woodruff, and Janina Wresh.

Thanks go to Cathy Spengler for her beautiful design, to Marly Cornell for her guidance and editing, and to Diane Keyes and Voncille Meyer for proofreading.

Cathy Paper has patiently managed a project that morphed from one concept to another. She's offered wise counsel, moral support, resources, contacts, and perspective. I'm proud to be a RockPaper-Star author.

I'm grateful to every person and organization who entrusted their stories to me. Though a select few appear in *Bitter or Better,* my website, www.carynmsullivan.com, includes all of my columns and blog posts.

To my family—Ted, Caitie, Peter, and Teddy Grace; Dan, Nicole, Baby A, and Baby B; Jack, Julia, and Chuck—it's been a crazy ride, but you've enriched my life and filled me with love, pride, and joy.

Discussion Questions

1. What is the greatest personal challenge you have faced?

2. When you experience adversity, do you speak of it with others?

3. How do you respond when people in your life experience difficulties?

4. What do you consider the most useful tool in the toolkit? Why?

5. After reading *Bitter or Better*, what might you do differently when someone in your life experiences adversity?

6. The author says it is as much a gift to accept an offer of help as to extend one. What are your thoughts?

7. Some people view the glass as half empty, others as half full. Which are you?

8. Have you thought about your legacy? Are you living it?

9. Do you believe that people can make fundamental changes in their outlook on life and their behavior? Why or why not?

10. The author writes about how words have helped her to heal. Have you experienced a different healing power?

11. What lesson(s) have you gleaned from *Bitter or Better* that you wish you had learned earlier in life?

12. In their eulogies, several children spoke about their fathers. What would your loved ones say about you?

13. Do you have a bucket list? Are you working on it? If not, what are you waiting for?

14. Are you living in the moment *and* planning for the future?

I am grateful for . . .

I'd like my legacy to be . . .

My bucket list includes . . .

Lessons gleaned from Bitter or Better . . .

Daily reminders . . .

Photo by Jim Fuglestad, March 26, 2005

Connecting

Bitter or Better is rich with material for reflection and discussion. Caryn is available to speak with groups of any size—from book clubs to conventions.

Contact her at caryn@carynmsullivan.com to book a speaking engagement.

Readers say Caryn's writing informs, illuminates, and inspires. Want to read more? Email her at caryn@carynmsullivan.com to join her mailing list. Peruse her writing portfolio at carynmsullivan.com.